Ba Duan Jin Qi Gong

Eduardo Barrios

DEDICATION

Wenceslao Eduardo Barrios
(13.09.1930-01.08.2020)

En memoria de Wenceslao Eduardo Barrios. Mi maestro, amigo, y padre. Descansa en paz mi querido viejo. Siempre estarás en nuestras memorias y corazones. Gracias por tus consejos y enseñanzas.

CONTENTS

八段錦氣

ACKNOWLEDGMENTS

I would like to thank Professor Li Yia Qing for sharing his Qi Gong Knowledge with me. I would also like to thank my children, and my students for their support and questioning that has helped me to become a better martial arts teacher.

Author's Foreword

In 1991, whilst studying Mechanical Engineering at Southbank University, I had the pleasure of meeting and training Qi Gong with Professor Li Yia Qing. Professor Li is an expert in Classical Chinese Literature as well as Yang Style Tai Chi and various Qi Gong methods. One of which was Ba Duan Jin Qi Gong.

Professor Li taught two methods of Ba Duan Jin the first methods was the commonly practiced method all around the world and the second was an enhanced Qi Gong routine which put greater emphasis on the movement of blood and Qi (vital energy). This method was once taught at the Nanjing Institute during the 1930's.

In this book, I introduce the enhanced second method, in addition to other simple exercises that have helped me to improve my health whilst recovering from a life saving operation and from two cerebral ischemic strokes over the last year.

The form shown in this book is considered as an External Qi Gong (Wei Dan Qi Gong-外丹 氣功) exercise, it is one of the treasures of Chinese Martial Arts and Health Restoring Exercises, with over 1000 years of practice by the Chinese nation. The 8 Strand of Brocade, are a complete set of Qi Gong exercises based on Traditional Chinese Medicine (TCM) Theory; containing meditation, breathing, body postures and gentle movements And smooth gentle and deep breathing.

Not only does Ba Duan Jin help to open and unblock the energy channels by regulating the San Jiao, but it also helps to reduce high blood pressure, improves blood circulation, and alleviates kidney problems and reduced stress levels by simply practicing eight simple exercises for ten to twenty-eight minutes per day; in a natural and relaxed manner over a prolonged period of time. In effect, Ba Duan Jin can improve cardiopulmonary function, relaxation, stress, improve sleep, and reduce the risks of ischemic strokes.

Each movement is designed to stretch the muscles, tendons and spine stimulating the meridians, internal organs and the cerebral cortex. By holding each position for a prolonged period of time, you increase the flow of blood throughout the body.

The form incorporates movements to further enhance the internal movement of blood and other nutrients by activating specific meridian (Gall Bladder, Kidney, Liver, Du Mai, spleen, stomach, lungs, pericardium and San Jiao for example) and specific acupressure points like Yong Quan (K1) at the base of your feet, Lou Gong (PC8) in the centre of your palms, Qi Hai at the lower abdomen and internal organs, which act as reservoirs of Qi for the body.

Although, the movements are simple in nature, they are powerful and profound in substance. Whilst practicing this exercise you may feel various sensations as the energy begins to move, and the flow of blood increases unblocking the arteries and veins.

You may feel tingling sensations, like ants moving up your spine, coldness in your body or limbs, one side hotter or colder in relationship to the other. These are indications of blood blockage or stagnation points along the channels and evidence that the Qi is trying to move and force open that particular area or channel. Occasionally, you may feel heaviness in your limbs when the Qi arrives or one side heavier than the other.

The action of the Ba Duan Jin form helps to regulate the liver, kidney, heart, spleen and lungs, other organs also benefit by the stretching action of the meridians related. But more specifically an anatomical division from the Chinese medicine point of view, known as San Jiao or Triple Heater is responsible for ensuring a free flow of Qi to the internal organs.

These divisions are the areas where internal organs are housed. They divide into lower Jiao at the lower abdomen where the lower Dantien is located, the middle Jiao where the stomach and epigastric region is located and the upper Jiao where the lungs and heart are housed. By activating the three Jiao's you can regulate the whole body from internal illness. Your health benefits by reducing high blood pressure stimulating kidney functions, releasing toxins through urination and perspiration.

I have done my best to be explicit with regards to the workings of the theories behind Ba Duan Jin Qi Gong as I understand it through my own qigong practice and study of Acupuncture, Tui-Na, Anatomy and Physiology.

Although, over the last few hundred years many variations of Ba Duan Jin have been created by traditional martial arts schools to further enhance the healing properties of this ancient exercise, there are two main distinct methods of practice that exist: Buddhist and Taoist Qi Gong Methods. However, they all have one point in common, that it improves your health and prolongs life.

I find that for martial training and to improve general health training, the standing methods are beneficial. The sitting method is more suitable for those wishing to achieve a more meditative state and for those physically indisposed due to illness.

In September 2006 I had a life saving operation which weakened my whole structure and one that cause long term damage to vital organs and blood circulation. I found that Ba Duan Jin and the other Qi Gong exercises shown in this book had gradually helped me to regain some of my inner strength and vitality allowing me to return to full time employment shortly after in June 2007. Medically, I was informed that I would never be able to practice any form of martial arts. As a martial artist and instructor I found this very difficult to deal with and accept, as it completely turned my world upside down. I found that, simply taking a walk brought tears to my eyes with every step, internal bleeding, and other side effects. A simple bus ride or trip to the shopping center or visit to the hospital for follow-up caused internal bleeding due to excessive vibration and force transference through my body.

In November 2009, I was given five year life expectancy with no chance for an organ transplant because the risk of the procedure far out-weight the benefits, too many risk and not cost effective, as a result I was given ill-health retirement. I had to take hold of the situation and look at ways to maintain a strong mind, so not to affect my family with worries. Also, to plan ahead with the time I was given, so as to try to improve my quality of life, and reduce stress levels.

I relied on my knowledge of Chinese martial arts, Qi Gong and Chinese Medicine to help to regain some quality of life. The first thing was to strengthen my body and mind through the practice of Ba Duan Jin and meditation. After six years of practicing Ba Duan Jin Qi Gong, I have become more resilient. I have recover some physical strength and able to exert some force, as required within Southern Praying Mantis training. I am not 100% and I doubt that it will ever overcome it, but I don't like giving up. Sometimes you need to set goals in your life to try to exceed your own expectations. I am still here, by the grace of God and Qi Gong.

I hope that you enjoy this humble effort to present to you this unique art of Qi Gong. Certainly, there may be better presented methods, which may be more appealing to you. However, based from my own experience I know that this method work. I am truly grateful, for having learned this ancient set of exercises from Professor Li Yia Qing.

Eduardo Barrios MAcS OA
6th Generation Master
Iron-Ox Praying Mantis

1 Background to Ba Duan Jin Qi Gong

General Yue Fei

It is believed that during the Song Dynasty (960-1279 AD) a General from humble origins by the name of Yue Fei (岳飛) was responsible for creating the art of Ba Duan Jin Qi Gong (八段錦氣功) usually termed as a Wei-Dan (外丹) or "External Elixir" in order to strengthen the bodies of his infantry men. Yue Fei is considered as its creator, his name is registered as the second inheritor of the Yi Jin Jing 易筋經 – The Sinew Changing Classic, at Shaolin.

Not only is he revered within the martial Arts as having created this Qi Gong method, but also with having created the art of Xing Ji Chuan from the art of spear play that he had learned in his youth. It is also believed that his art of grabbing and locking became Eagle Claw Boxing 108 Locking methods.

To the Chinese nation Yue Fei is considered as a hero, representing righteousness and justice. A mausoleum was built in Hanzhao, Zhejian, to commemorate him.

What is Qi?

Qi (氣) is perhaps the most fundamentals essence in life, it exist in every living-breathing organism. In relation to Qi Gong, Qi refers to the body's ability to transform energy via the three heaters, the San Jiao. The San Jiao consist of three cavities: lower Jiao relates to the Kidney vessel, the middle Jiao to the stomach and Spleen vessel and the upper Jiao to the lung.

氣
功

Even by looking at the Chinese character for Qi it implies transformation of matter and energy. The Qi radical is made up two components: the simplified character for vital energy, Qi (气) and the character for rice grain (米); the change from a solid state to a gas and steam. That is Qi.

I have already mentioned previously that the Chinese term the life energy Qi (氣). This Qi is linked to the Streams, brooks, rivers, seas and the oceans of mother Earth, the carriers of life. We, in the western world may refer to these relationships as arteries, veins, capillaries, cells, or systems (respiratory, circulatory, endocrine, nervous, lymphatic, etc) all working in perfect harmony to maintain a healthy and strong body.

What is Qi Gong?

Qi Gong is an ancient practice of energy exercises used to improve the blood and vital energy flow, which is over 5,000 years old.

QI Vital Energy Transformation	
Matter (Food, liquids) 米	Energy (Gas, steam) 气

It integrates physical postures, breathing techniques, and focused intention. The word Qi Gong (氣功) is made up of two Chinese characters. 氣 (pronounced "chee") is usually

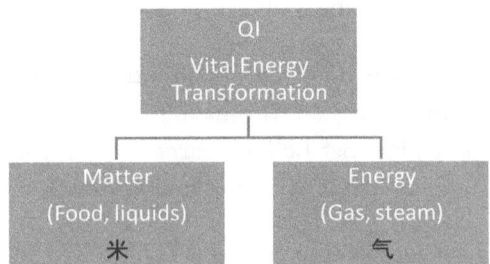

translated to mean the life force or the vital energy that flows through all things in the universe.

The second word, 功 (pronounced "gung") means accomplishment, work or skill that is cultivated though consistent practice. Together, Qi Gong implies the cultivation of vital energy or prana as practiced in yoga.

There are many sets or styles of Qi Gong designed for the practiced of health maintenance, healing, increasing vitality, physical strength and spiritual cultivation. Ba Duan Jin Qi Gong is one such method that helps to strengthen and restored the body's energy.

What are the benefits?

One of the benefits of Ba Duan Jin Qi Gong as a health restoring exercise is that it can be practiced by anyone. This practice has shown to lower blood pressure, increase blood circulation, improve digestion, increase cardiovascular strength and reduce stress levels.

In my situation, it helped me to regain my inner strength, improved my blood flow, slowly, helped me to regain muscular strength and muscle tone. It helped me to focus and deal with my anxieties and reduced stress.

These gentle, slow movements are especially geared for those people with injuries, chronic conditions, and reduced flexibility, to enable them to gain greater mobility and physical strength.

Furthermore, Ba Duan Jin can strengthen the muscular-skeletal system by bringing energy to the limbs, and strengthening soft tissue and internal organs, specially the kidney, heart, liver, spleen and lungs. Although, by activating the meridians all the Zang and Fu organs are also stimulated (see chapter 2). You need to understand to the Chinese mind and TCM, illnesses are a product of imbalances of Yin-Yang.

Here the Zang Fu plays an important aspect in the practice of Ba Duan Jin because each position activates specific number of organs with the aim to regulate the Qi flow to and from the internal organs.

Who is it for?

Ba Duan Jin Qi Gong is for everyone, regardless of personal abilities or age, because Ba Duan Jin is a low impact type of breathing exercises, which is easy on the knees, simple in movements, it has a few physical and cognitive demands, making ideal to learn and practice by anyone.

Even, if you are not fit and healthy, it should not stop you from practicing this Qi Gong. It is better to prevent a disease, than to try to cure it.

For those with chronic conditions or recuperating from injuries, Ba Duan Jin can lessen or eliminate their symptoms with consistent Qi Gong practice. If anything, it helps to improve your quality of life.

However, prior to committing to do any of these exercises you should consult with a medical expert in charge of your condition, especially if you have just undergone some form of surgery, just to be on the safe side. We are all unique human beings and ones person medical condition may not be the same to someone else with the same condition due to various factors such as age, initial physical estate, the frame of mind etc.

There is a warning for ladies going through pregnancy; Ba Duan Jin should not be practiced by anyone during any stage of pregnancy, to avoid the risk of miscarriage.

Place the tip of the tongue on the upper ridge of the teeth.

When practicing this qigong it is not necessary to practice visualization to direct the Qi. What is important is to breathe as natural, as deep and as relaxed as possible, ensuring that the tip of your tongue touches slightly your upper palate or behind the ridge of your teeth. The physical postures of Qi Gong promote both natural structural tension of the muscles and relaxation to Re-energize the body.

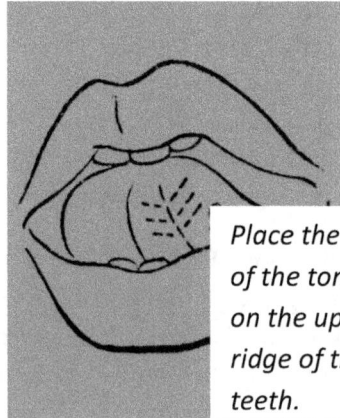

How Qi works?

In order to understand how Qi Gong is able to achieve a free flow of Qi in the body, imagine a basic electric circuit with a light bulb connected to it - the current flows freely if there is no resistance obstructing the current flow in the circuit. Then, the light bulb will be bright.

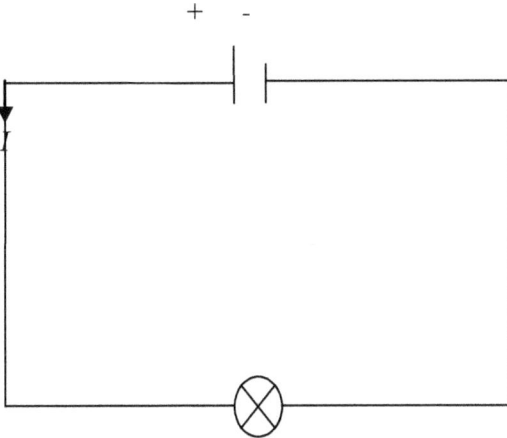

If there is a resistor or a brake in the circuit, current (Qi) doesn't flow freely; therefore, reducing the current flow. Hence, eventually leading the light bulb to become deemed and eventually burning out, leading to ill-health. Likewise, if an artery is blocked with a blood clot the flow of blood will be impeded affecting internal organs and damaging your health and even threatening life.

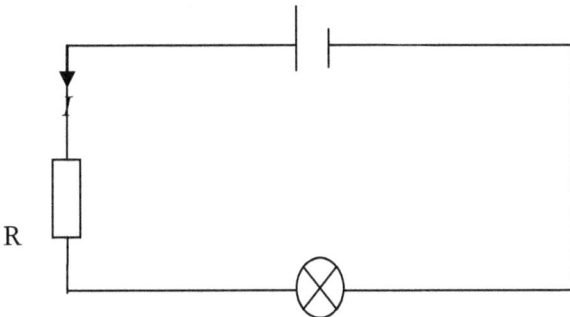

When this happens, you get excess (Qi) on one side of the circuit and deficiency on the other (causing a voltage drop on the affected side of the circuit). The stretching, movements and breathing of Qigong elongate the connections reducing the resistance and releases the blockages caused by trauma, stress, poor diet, medications, environmental factors or excessive emotional issues. Maintaining an even flow of bio-energy or Qi assures the health of your internal organs, nerves, glands and cells by stimulating the body's natural ability to heal itself.

However, unlike the simplified electric circuit analogy above, the human body is much complex than that. For example, it is said that Qi in the human body comes from the essence of your parents, hence, Pre-natal Qi or Jing which is stored in the kidneys. However Qi can also be store in the digested food that we consume, normally called Gu Qi, where the spleen moves the Gu Qi from food essence up to the lungs combining with gathering o clear Qi which in turns leads to Zong Qi or the acquired Qi after birth.

In essence, Zong Qi it is about the exchange of oxygen and carbon-dioxide from the body. By fully expelling all the carbon-dioxide from the lungs, you improve cellular breathing with fresh oxygenated blood. And therefore the organs will have a richer blood supply; inducing to better health.

I think I should talk about the act of breathing itself, as a separate section. It is important because Qi Gong is all about breathing methods. Essentially there two different breathing methods in Chinese Qi Gong exercises. These are known as the Buddhist (normal) and the Taoist (reverse) breathing methods. We will look at it next.

Breathing Methods

In the western world, most people do not use their lungs to full capacity. We normally tend to use only the top of our lungs. Some people like deep sea free-divers for example they can use every ounce of their lung capacity. They have a greater breath, mind-control and cellular breathing that allow them to reach a vertical descent of over two-hundred meters and holding their breaths for at least ten minutes or more. Mere mortals like us we never get anywhere within those levels of atmospheric pressures. That crushes your lungs with every ten meters of depth.

However, what I find amazing about this sport is the single mindedness, the high level of dedication and consistency. Now, if we compared the breath and mind-control Chinese Qi Gong exercises demand and the sense of feeling at one with the universe is the same feeling that free divers experience. They have to be unified with their minds and body. The body has to be relaxed; the minds calm, the breath soft, deep and slow; reducing the heart rate. Where the free-divers learn to master a single breath to rich those depths there is some physiological action taking place that's not fully understood by western science, just like the concept of Qi itself.

Coordinating the inhalation and exhalation process with the contracting and expanding movements of the abdominal cavity; gently massaging the internal organs forcing fresh blood to flow in and out of each organ induces for better blood circulation throughout the whole body.

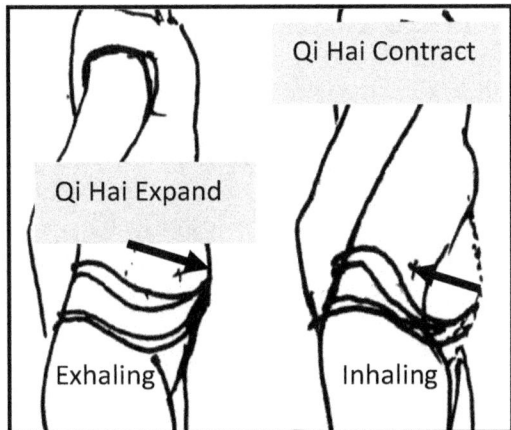

Think back to when a fetus is in the mother's womb, the fetus is breathing from the umbilical cord. In essence it is practicing abdominal breathing.

Taoist Breathing

In Chinese Qi Gong therefore, the aim is to revert our bodies to that initial stage, of pre-birth. The two breathing methods use to enhance our vital energy and bring our bodies back to feel that sense of calmness are the Buddhist (normal breathing) and Taoist (reverse breathing) as mentioned previously. However, they both focus on Dan Tien Breathing.

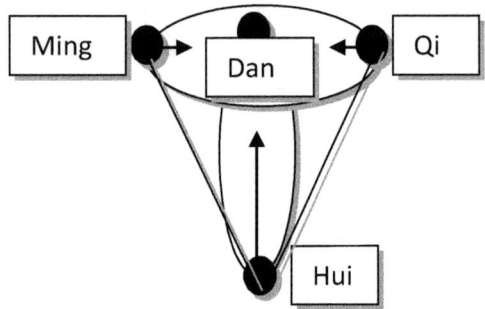

The breathing patterns mechanics are different to each other. The Buddhist breathing can be compared to when you inhale the lower abdomen expands and at exhaling the lower abdomen contracts.

Dan Tien Breathing

One of the unique skills which are fundamental to both methods of breathing is the strengthening of the Dan Tien (丹田) in the lower abdomen. The aim is to build the fire (Qi) in the lower abdomen, to store the energy. In order to do this the breathing is coordinated with the lifting of the perineum at point Hui Yin (a point located between the anus and the scrotum on the pelvic floor) and the contracting and expansion of the Ming Men (at 2nd lumbar vertebra) and Qi Hai (two fingers below the umbilicus) vital points. See diagram aside. This action strengthens the lower Dan Tien and activates the Dai Mai belt. This is the extraordinary meridian which acts as a Qi reservoir for the body, depicted by the grey circle in the diagram above.

The Dai Mai has the function of binding all the energetic channels passing through the body that we call meridians (Jingluo).

The second circle is referred to as the Micro-orbit circulation. The lesser circulation than the protective Wei Qi circulation that runs up through the center of the spine and the front of the body from the Hui Yin to the head meeting at Ren Zhong point on the upper ridge of your teeth, normally known as Small Circulation in Qi Gong.

When focusing in practicing the cultivation of Qi, the breath has to be natural smooth, deep and relaxed with full exhalation. Here is important to adopt one specific breathing method mentioned earlier.

For example when you inhale and the stomach contracts, sense how the perineum floor lifts and the Qi Hai (the sea of energy point) and Ming Men (the life gate point) tend to meet in the center of the abdomen, creating a warming sensation. This is the beginning of Qi activation.

In the Taoist Breathing- when you inhale the lower abdomen contracts and the Qi Hai moves towards the Ming Men, simultaneously lifting the perineum at point Hui Yin; when exhaling the stomach expands and the perineum prolapsed. The latter breathing method has greater benefits for martial artist and Qi Gong as a whole, it can be said that it can:

- Strengthen the abdominal walls
- Relaxes the mind and body
- Strengthen immune system by improving the protection Qi (Wei Qi).
- Helps the body with the function of greater exchanging incoming fresh oxygen with outgoing carbon-dioxide.
- Slow down the heart beat
- Lowers and stabilizes blood pressure
- Lower stress levels
- Strengthens the Dan Tien (Lower Heaven) strengthening the mind and body as a result.

The Moderation Rule

As previously stated, breathing should be calm and not forced, to avoid stagnation. However, in order to maximize lung capacity one should aim to breathe to a point where one feels comfortable, say to 70% of your capacity. If you feel too tight at the chest you are over doing it. You are over exerting yourself. This also means not to exert too much force to the point where you are totally tense and not to be totally limp, but to have natural tension to activate the fascia. For example, by gently spreading your fingers and opening the fingers at the web, as if you were holding small marbles between your fingers, but not stiff.

In relation to exhaling and inhaling, one should not hold the breath in between cycles in order to avoid excess tension or stress. And the tip of the tongue should naturally touch the upper ridge of the teeth of the upper palate.

Moderation in Qigong also refers to your quality of life, your diet (good quality and healthy foods), work, rest, alcohol consumption and sexual desires. All these can have a direct effect on your Qi and your overall health.

Here, the kidney function is important, because it is said that the essence Qi resides in the Kidneys. Therefore, having strong and healthy kidneys and liver it can lead to a healthy and long life. According to Chinese medical theories, overindulgence in sexual activities can lead to weakness of your kidney function causing Yin Qi deficiency; in other words decreasing your sexual drive as a result.

The Purpose of Qi Gong

The aim of any good Qi Gong exercise is to regulate three basic elements or core properties, which Ba Duan Jin definitely meet:

1. To regulate the body

2. To regulate the breath

3. To regulate the mind

Ba Duan Jin cover all three purposes, the body is regulated by practicing controlled relaxed breathing, supported by gentle physical movement, which stimulate the blood flow through the arteries and veins and calming the Mind.

It is said, that Qi has two main aspects, namely, sense and function. This refers to:

1. Refine essence, produced by the internal organs that nourish the body, mind and spirit.

2. The functional activity of the internal organs.

There is a close relationship between the Qi and the blood (血, Xue); in fact the blood may be considered as a form of Qi. There are four main aspects or properties to these relationships:

- *Qi originates blood*
- *Qi moves the blood*
- *Qi holds the blood*
- *Blood nourishes the Qi*

This is important to comprehend, that from the Chinese medical point of view, there are three basic pathological blood states that can affect health. These are shown as blood deficiency, heat and stasis. These can make themselves present along any meridian or channel, thus, altering the balance between yin and Yang. This creates a weakness in the pertaining internal organ, causing ill health. To restore a Qi balance, it is essential to treat the body immediately, and not leave the injury to settle for a long time, as it will give rise to secondary problems. Ba Duan Jin Qi Gong can assist in maintaining the body in good health and restoring a free flow of Qi.

I would like to stop at this point and direct you to the next Chapter, as it describes the relationship between the blood, Qi and its flow in relation to the internal organs. I believe, that understanding the flow of Qi throughout the body, will provide you with greater benefits when practicing any Qi Gong form. This type of knowledge is often reserved for Traditional Chinese Doctors and Chinese Martial Arts Masters. I hope you find this effort beneficial to you. What I am proposing in this book it is from my own understanding and practice, it is definitely not the only way to look at Ba Duan Jin nor is it the best way, but it is the most logical way in my mind.

You will find that within the Li Yia Qin method of Ba Duan Jin that comes from the Nan Jing Kuoshu Institute in the 1930's. The method it is slightly different from the typical Shoaling based Ba Duan Jin methods shown. In this method position 1 and position 4 are the most powerful. Position one function is to open the flow of Qi throughout the whole body and all meridians, therefore to achieve this you need to understand the San Jiao (三焦) and Zang Fu theory which is the main focus in Chapter Two. Position four further enhances brain wave activity, and stimulates the cerebral cortex and both sides of the brain hemisphere.

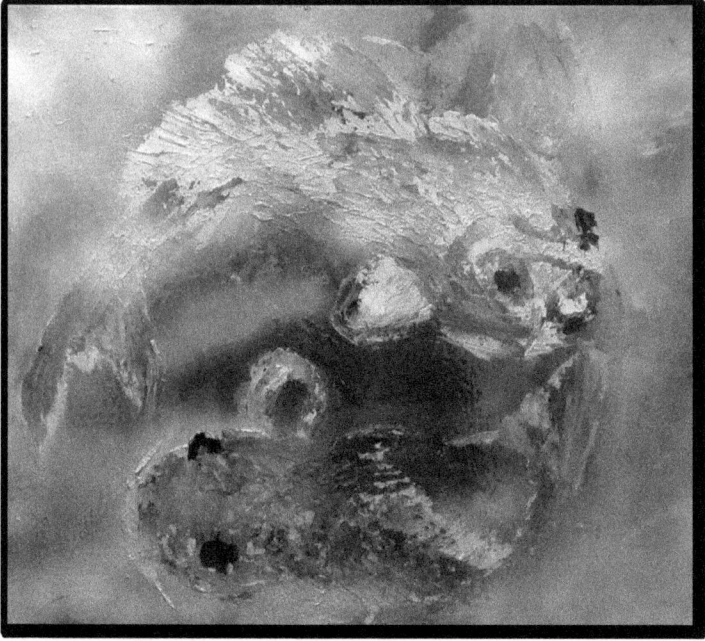

Yin-Yang

Yin-Yang are the two universal forces that cause everything to exist. The Yin is considered the passive and the Yang the active force. However, they both have dualistic properties within each other as in life. In the painting above the Yin-Yang and Wuqi concepts are embodied, one carps chase the other in a continuous harmonious circle, representing harmony and the Tao. The artwork is courtesy of the author: Yin-Yang, mixed media on canvas. Acrylics, Metallic paint and epoxy resin.

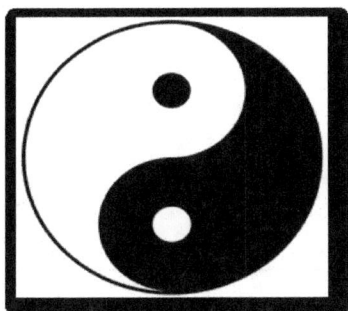

2 Relationships to San Jiao & Zang Fu

This life force (氣) that we have been speaking about, is present in all living things, (if you are able to breathe, then you have it), is like electricity. It flows in a current, and though we cannot actually see it, we can feel the manifestation of it, and the effects of it. In a way, it is like the blood flowing through our veins which, we usually do not see it, but feel it pulsating life through us all. However, according to Chinese medicine, it is believed that, Qi has five main functions, these are: pushing, warming, defending, controlling and transforming. But the Qi nourish via the blood (cellular breathing).

Once this flow fails, diseases set in. Health and illness are defined by this life energy. It is this energy that Traditional Chinese Doctors and Qi Gong practitioners speak of balancing if some aspect of this energy is no longer in harmony with the totality. These are normally considered as imbalances of the San Jiao (三焦), since the sanjiao it is also responsible for regulating the fluid in the body as well as the free flow of Qi in the body.

The Five Weaknesses & Seven Injuries

In Chinese medicine sometimes it is referred as the 5 weakness and the 7 injuries. Here the five weaknesses are related to the illness of the five main organs and the seven injuries; refer to the seven emotions related to the five organs.

Five Weaknesses	Seven Injuries
Heart	Joy
Liver	Anger
Kidney	Fear, love
Lungs	Grief
Spleen	Anxiety, Worry

Internal imbalances occur due to over indulgence or over exertion of the seven emotions. Excess sadness and grief can create an imbalance in the lung Qi. However, and imbalance in the kidney can lead to Oedema, high blood pressure a weaken heart and in time to fluid retention in the lungs.

It can be seen that from the Ba Duan Jin Qi Gong point of view the correct functioning of the five internal viscera's is important to health, but a greater focus is placed on strengthening the kidneys, liver, pericardium and lungs to strengthen the Qi and regulate the San Jiao (三焦).

Yin-Yang

Qi Gong practitioners and Chinese Doctors all believe that Qi energy flows through pathways called meridians and that internal organs are connected via these meridians.

Basically, these channels or pathways are divided into two groups, defined by their Yin (陰) and Yang (陽) characteristics. (Refer to the Zang Fu Theory). Where Yang represents light, day or the sun, and the Yin represents darkness, the night or the moon; the body's surfaces it is also divided into its yin-yang correlations. For example the right side is considered Yang, and therefore it refers to the Qi. The left, the Yin side it refers to Xue (blood). In addition the inside of the body is considered yin, the outside yang, the top yang, the bottom yin, the back yang the front yin. The channels are divided into Yin-Yang and therefore each position in Ba Duan Jin stimulated and relates to specific yin and yang vessels.

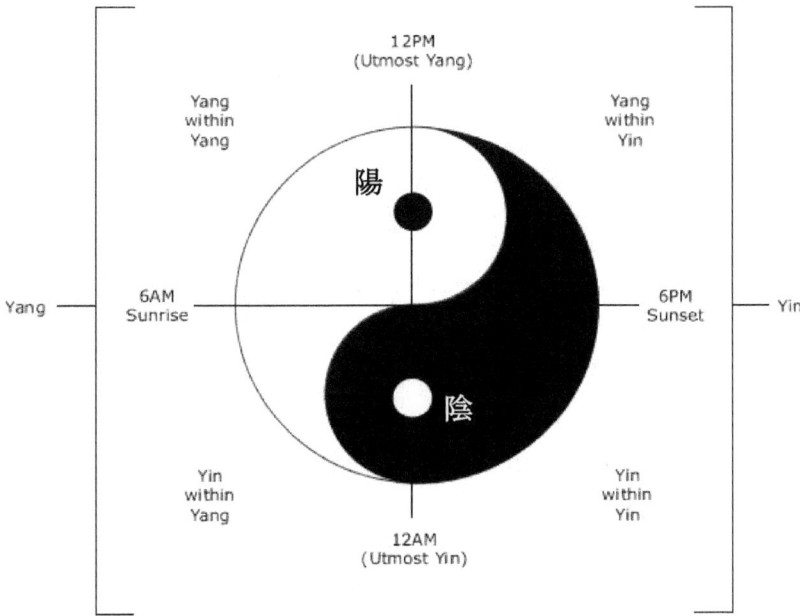

The 24 hrs Yin-Yang Cycle

It can be said that the body follows the rhythms of the moon, and that therefore the different cycles of the moon will affect the human body in terms of energy flow. The body is mostly water; therefore it must obey the laws of nature, where the moon's gravitational force acts on the oceans of the world causing lunar tides. This tidal changes.it must also act on the body's blood circulation. Let's say that high tide occurs at 12 noon, then that would imply that the heart will be experiencing a maximum blood flow and activity at midday and also at midnight. However, there will also be two low tides during the 24h. To simplified this concept of tidal flow of blood and Qi in the body, martial artist and Chinese medicine practitioner come to the concept of dividing the body into Three Gates (Sam Lo) or Three Heaters (San Jiao), which tracks the flow of Qi and blood through the day and its physical phase changes from yin to yang estates (see San Jiao).

The Qi flows through the body in a daily cycle that consists of a 12 hour period. Where, one period is equal to two hours each, within our 24 hour day.

Each period relates to a specific meridian. There are 12 pathways in the body (meridians) through which the energy flows, there are also eight extraordinary meridians of which the Du Mai, Ren Mai and Dai Mai are very important to the practice of Qi Gong These relate to the Micro-Orbit Circulation and the Dan Tien Breathing. The 12 meridians are divided in to their Yin-Yang components. Six channels are considered Yin and six are Yang. This helps to outline the flow of Qi throughout the body (see Zang Fu Theory).

Yin-Yang, the two universal forces are represented by a circle and within this circle there are two 'fish' like figures chasing each other in an endless cycle of creation and destruction, as shown above.

The circle represents "the universe", while the black and white shapes within the circle represent the inter-action of two energies called Yin (black) and Yang (white), which causes everything to exist. Yin is considered the passive, negative force, and Yang the active, positive force. In terms of Chinese medicine, the Yin-Yang is the primary substances, where Qi is considered Yang (vital, active, and energetic) and Blood is considered Yin (fluid, nourishing, substantial).

When there are imbalances of Yin and Yang, it accounts for the development of bad health, leading to all kind of diseases or illnesses. Therefore, Ba Duan Jin exercises can help to regulate the Zang Fu by directly regulating the San Jiao which in turn helps to strengthen the vessels. See the following section for more detail information on the San Jiao. Since the first position in Ba Duan Jin is design to fully regulate the San Jian and the smooth flow of Qi in and out of the viscera's, I cannot just leave it out.

I know, that this book is perhaps too heavy on the medical side, and it may not be what most people may be looking for, but Ba Duan Jin was developed with Chinese Medical Theory, therefore to really understand and benefit from it you need to understand the physiology that's involved in it.

The only way I know how to explain it. My understanding of the San Jiao is more than cavity, it has its own function, its own energy, it converts substances, it allows for a free transportation of energy Qi and Jin essence to the organs.

The San Jiao

San Jiao (三焦) it is primarily, a concept from traditional Chinese medicine, where the body is divided into three areas or heat exchangers, namely the upper, middle and lower heater, each paired to a Fu type organ.

The upper burner deals primarily with the lungs and heart, the middle burner with the liver, spleen, stomach, kidneys and gall bladder and the lower burner with the large intestine, small intestine, and bladder.

In reference to Ba Duan Jin Qi Gong the San Jiao aims to synthesize and distribute the Qi energy throughout the body and organs. Therefore, the first four position of the Ba Duan Jin Qi Gong are specifically designed to foster Qi circulation to the internal organs and to restore the yin-yang balance in the body. Therefore, opening the Qi in all the channels and removing blockages by increasing a free flow of Qi to all the organs in the San Jiao.

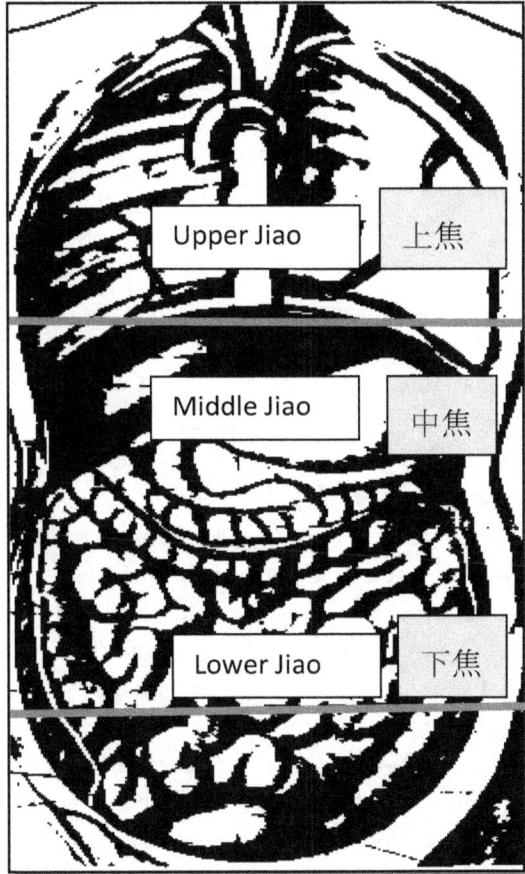

When the San Jiao is balanced, then, the body will be healthy. San Jiao permits Qi to pass freely and smoothly throughout the body. It strengthens the organs, permitting Qi to flow smoothly to and from the organs. The body and tendons are therefore strengthening through the practice of Ba Duan Jin externally; but internally all the organs, the blood, fluids and nutrients benefit from the practice of Ba Duan Jin. Hence, train the internal through stillness, and the external: the muscles and tendons through movement.

The importance of the first position in Ba Duan Jin merits further information. Hence, Buddha Holding 300 Catties or Holding the Heavens as it is also known; implies the lifting of the arm over the head with intent. The first name is more descriptive as it gives you an idea of the intent, because 300 catties are equivalent to 180 kg approximately.

Also position one, enhances the free flow of Qi to all meridians, regulating the sanjiao and body fluids.

Buddha holding Three-hundred Catties

Buddha Holding a Three-Hundred Catties (180kg) is the first position of Ba Duan Jin Qi Gong. It is also known as, 'Holding the Heavens'. It resembles a man lifting and holding a heavy weight of gold. However, in Ba Duan Jin the weight is visualized as it helps to direct intent and the energy to the Arms. When you lift your weight onto the ball of your feel you activate the kidney meridian at point 1 of the kidney channel at a point called Yong Quan. More importantly, this position stretches all the connecting meridians activating the San Jiao that help and balance all the internal organs and fluid within the body.

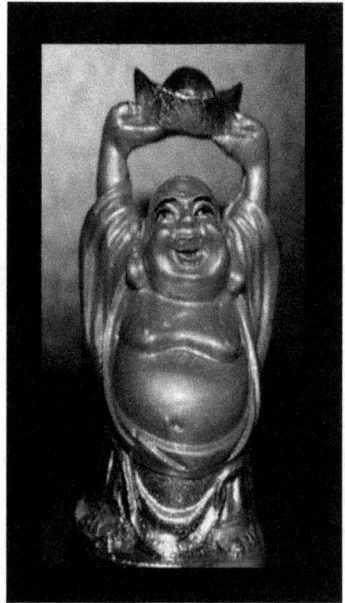

The first position of Ba Duan Jin Qi Gong shown aside stimulates all the channels and collaterals of the body, and helps to increase and open or unblock stagnated energy within the veins and arteries. Therefore, strengthening the whole body and increasing the blood flow in addition to regulating the San Jiao.

The San Jiao within martial arts also depicts the subdivision of the body into the three gates (literally the upper, middle and lower gates) where the border of the upper Jiao and the border of the lower Jiao mark the same border divisions of the Three Gates, Sam Lo/ Sam Mun (三門) this in turn relates to the three phase cycle of the Qi through the body. For more details, look at the Classical Order of the Meridians and the Three Phase Cycle.

When the San Jiao is balanced the Qi can flow free to-and-from the organs. So in effect this position can help to cure many diseases, or at the very least help to prevent what is considered in Chinese medicine as the five weaknesses and the seven injuries. These refer to the illness of the five yin organs (heart, liver, spleen, kidney and lungs) and to the seven basic emotions or feelings (anger, fear, anxiety, joy, grief, worry, and love) that are associated to its corresponding internal organ as mentioned at the beginning of chapter two. I don't think we can talk about the Zang Fu and the San Jiao without making passing references to the idea of Wuxing or Five Element Theory. According to this ancient theory organs are coupled in relation to their element, activity, time factor, season etc.

Coupled Organs:

1. Liver-Gallbladder
2. Spleen-Stomach
3. Heart-Small Intestine
4. Lungs-Large Intestine
5. Kidneys-Bladder

The Ancient Energy Flow Pathway

It is believed that the Qi flows in the following order and pathway according the paired organs.

a. First, the Liver and Gallbladder are most active
b. Second, the Spleen and the Stomach are most active
c. Third, the Heart and Small Intestine are most active
d. Fourth, the Lungs and Large Intestine are most active
e. Fifth, the Kidney and the Bladder are most active

Each Zang organ has a specific season related to it and a particular element. It will become more apparent in the Zang Fu Theory on the next page.

a. The Liver is most active in Spring
b. The Heart(Pericardium) is more active in Summer
c. The Spleen is most active in late summer
d. The lungs is most active in the Autumn
e. The Kidneys are most active during winter.

Zang (臟) Fu (腑) Theory

In a simplistic way, this theory shows that the meridians connect and relate to the internal organs, via the six yin and six yang meridians. These organs sometimes are referred to as the six-solid and the six-hollow organs. Physiologically, the yin type organs tend to store vital energy or Qi and these are referred to Zang (臟). Each of these organs has its own energy type according to the Five Element Theory, as shown in the table below. The yang type organs are referred as Fu (腑) organs and they have the ability of transmitting energy throughout the body, but do not retain or store energy.

Zang Fu Table.

Element	Zang (臟) Store Energy	Fu (腑) Transmit Energy
Metal 金	Lung 肺	Large Intestine 大肠
Earth 土	Spleen 脾	Stomach 胃
Fire 火	Heart 心	Small Intestine 小肠
Water 水	Kidneys 肾	Urinary Bladder 膀胱
Wood 木	Liver 肝	Gall Bladder 胆
Fire 火	Pericardium 心包	Triple Warmer 三焦

The Classical Order of Meridians

According, to the traditional Chinese idea of the cycle of Qi within the Meridians, the Chinese determined that the energy flows from one meridian to the next in a continuous and fixed order, with its associated organ.

It flows from meridian to meridian in a two-hour cycle, during these periods the Qi is at its maximum energy, within that channel and organ. A complete circuit is performed once a day. The flow of energy begins with the Meridians of the Lungs and completes its full cycle within the Liver, to commence again at the Lungs, continuing the daily cycle throughout an individual's life span. At this point, it is important to understand that, the Qi flows in a pre-arranged sequence and in a three-phase cycle.

MERIDIAN	ENTRY-EXIT POINT	BI-Hourly Period
Lungs	L1-L7	3 to 5 AM
Large Intestines	LI4-LI20	5 to 7 AM
Stomach	ST1-ST42	7 to 9 AM
Spleen	SP1-SP21	9 to 11 AM
Heart	H1-H9	11 to 13 PM
Small Intestine	SI1-SI19	13 to 15 PM
Bladder	UB1-UB67	15 to 17 PM
Kidney	K1-K22	17 to 19 PM
Pericardium	PC1-PC8	19 to 21 PM
San Jiao	SJ1-SJ22	21 to 23 PM
Gall Bladder	GB1-GB41	23 TO 1 AM
Liver	LV1-LV14	1AM to 3AM

The Three-Phase Cycle & the Yin Qi Flow

In the human body, there are three main Qi phase cycles, and three yin meridians that run along the inner side of the arms and legs; and three yang meridians on the outside of the arms, and three Yang on the outside of the legs. All the channels relate to the Yin Qi flow. The Yin Qi corresponds to the tracking of the sun throughout the 24 hour day. As mentioned previously it remains for two hours in each vessel.

The three-phase cycle, also refers to traditional Chinese Martial Arts, whereby, the body is divided into three gates (Sam-Lo) marking the direction of the Qi flow through the 24 hour day. Each phase consists of 8 hours, and each cycle has four meridians through which the Qi flows before leaving or entering the next vessel. This implies that each of the 12 meridians shown in the phases below, correspond to a two hour cycle, in which a meridian will have a maximal Qi and blood flow through it. After the two hour period is up, the Qi flow will become a maximal flow at the next meridian down the connecting chain of meridians, entering at a gate point or connecting point.

For example the sun at midday corresponds to Yin Qi moving to the heart, the Yin Qi remains approximately 2 hours in the heart. At sunset, it moves to the pericardium vessel.

It is common for the Yin Qi Cycle to suffer blockages and stagnation of energy and blood between the spleen and heart vessels from spleen point 21 to Heart point 1; also between the liver and lungs vessels at liver point 14 to lung 1 point.

The path is shown in the table below for each cycle:

Phase 1 (upper gate): Lungs (3 AM to 5 AM) to Large Intestine (5 AM to 7AM) to Stomach (7 AM to 9 AM) to Spleen (9 AM to 11 AM).
Phase 2 (middle gate): Heart (11 AM to 1 PM) to Small Intestine (1 PM to 3 PM) to Bladder (3 PM to 5 PM) to Kidney (5 PM to 7 PM).
Phase 3 (lower gate): Pericardium (7 PM to 9 PM) to San Jiao (9 PM to 11 PM) to Gall Bladder (11 PM to 1 AM) to Liver (1 AM to 3 AM).

The 3rd and final cycle constitutes a full Qi cycle within a 24 hours period terminating at the liver, ready to commence fresh again at the lungs.

Diagrams Distribution of the 3 Yin Channels of the Arms & Legs

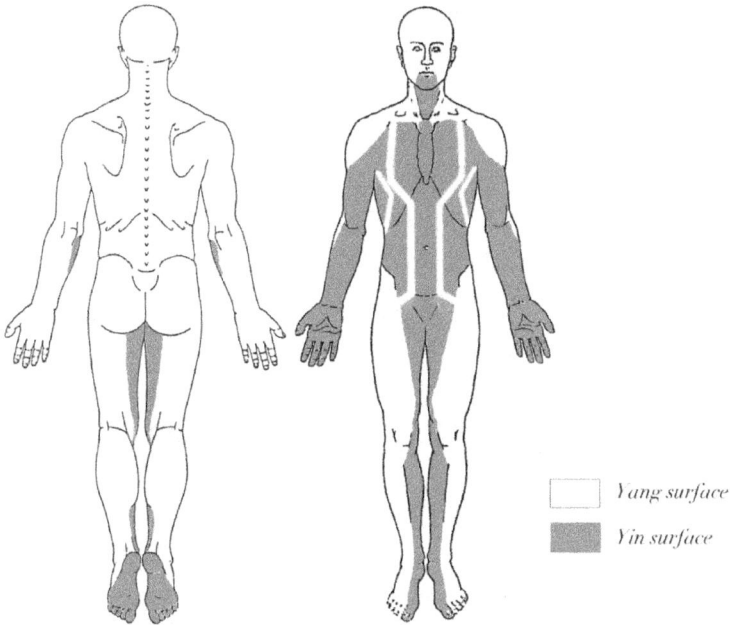

Yang surface

Yin surface

In respect to Yin & Yang above the body also have its sun and moon properties. Literally anywhere where the sun don't shine is considered Yin, anywhere where the sun touches the surface is considered yang in nature. So all the white and bright surfaces are yang, likewise the right of the body is considered yang according to the 24 hours yin-yang cycle. Where the Qi is yang and the blood is considered Ying.

Lung

Heart

Pericardium

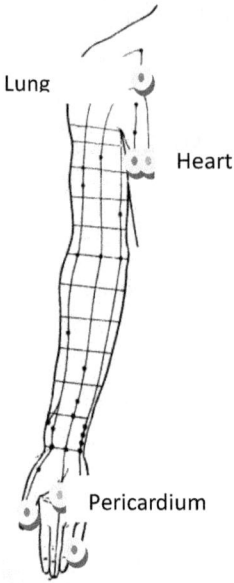

The diagram aside shows the relative position of the three yin channels of the arm. The channels star at the chest and end in the finger tips. The lung channel runs on the outside edge of the inner arm, along the radius and the heart channel, the opposite side along the ulna bone. The pericardium channel follows the path of the median nerve along the middle of the arm.

3 Guidelines for Practicing Ba Duan Jin Qi Gong

I have found that the best way to practice Ba Duan Jin Qi Gong is to find a place, where you can be relaxed, calm and undisturbed. A surrounding with fresh air and green colors are ideal. . When practicing Qi Gong your breathing should be smooth and natural. Not forced. Each position should be held for as long as physically possible in a relaxed and balanced posture. You can practice one position at a time, or the whole set, according to your needs.

Should visualization be used when practicing Qi Gong in the early stages? I believe that at the initial stages is not absolutely necessary. It is more important that the body be relaxed and not totally void of energy at this stage. Ensure to maintain the body straighten, shoulders dropped, hands at the sides, fingers slightly separated apart breathing from the lower abdomen, inhaling through the nose and out through the mouse and nose; contracting the abdomen as you inhale. As you inhale subconsciously lift the perineum in a slow and relaxed manner. When you exhale Hui Yin prolapsed.

At a later stage, you may which to use your mind to direct the flow of energy to the body following the meridians paths. In specific the Yin channels paths.

There are risks of blocking your own Qi if you force the flow without ensuring that the Qi is sunk to the Dan Tien. On occasions, when the individual is too much in a hurry these things can occur, normally the Qi would remain in the head, causing headaches, and nose bleed. When there is excess Qi in the liver due to lack of proper sleep for example your eyes may feel like burning or reddish.

However, sometimes there is 'good pain' associated with the practice of qigong. This can happen when the Qi and blood has reached a point in a meridian or an area where there is a previous injury, an old injury, blood stagnation or Qi stagnation. As I said before the blood has three different properties and it can manifest itself as heat, Stasis and deficiency of blood.

It is easier for you to feel the side effects of blood stagnation and heat in your body than blood deficiency. For example due to trauma, you may feel swelling and heat in an area. Bruising or deep pain within soft tissue when you touch the area you may feel a hard lump, this is often due to stagnation.

Ba Duan Jin can help to bring the Zang Fu into balance, restoring health if you are ill, and preventing illnesses if you are not.

Points for attention:

- To relax your body of all physical tension
- To subconsciously put all prevailing thoughts aside
- To keep your back straight and head erect as if it were suspended from a string; naturally aligning your body and decreasing tension in your overall posture. Therefore, increasing a free flow of Qi.
- To take natural and smooth and deep breath to your lower Dan Tien (the lower elixir of essence), also known as Qi Hai or the sea of energy, a point 3" below the umbilicus. The breath should become a very perceptible nasal breathe.
- Inhale as you begin your upward movement. Exhale as you begin the downward movement.
- Hold each posture for a few minutes increasing the length of time as your body increases in strength. Don't forget to breath.
- To help you relax and calm your emotions gently form an inner smile by relaxing the corners of your mouth. This will help to strengthen the liver, increasing the vitality of the organ and therefore, increasing the flow of vital energy and blood.
- Practice each position, individually at first, then, practice the full set. You can focus on an individual exercise for a particular ailment.
- You can train each position for a few minutes or the whole set within ten minutes.

However, I suggest that you practice position one and two at first in conjunction with your chosen form, as it will help to regulate the San Jiao, as explained previously, and in return open all the meridians in your body, increasing blood flow and energy to your internal organs. You must note that all breathing is nasal and the mouth is kept close to:

- Place the tip of your tongue on the upper ridge of your palate to create a connecting bridge between the Du and Ren meridian, at Ren Zhong (see related acupuncture points on last chapter).
- Be persistent in your training and within 3 months you will taste the Qi, if not sooner.
- Practice twice daily: early morning and evening, each time for at least 10 to 30 minutes. Increase the amount of exercise gradually.
- As time goes by use abdominal breathing, ensure the breath is even and smooth.
- Warm up prior to exercise to avoid soft tissue damage and cool the body down at the end of the exercise.
- You can take a relaxed walk to get the blood moving and gradually bring the body to rest. You can practice the following cooling down methods: gentle wrist rotation, arm swinging from side to side, patting the arms, chest, buttocks, and thighs with your palm softly. Massage your face, from the temples to the top of the head and down to the back of the neck.

What you may feel when practicing Ba Duan Jin Qi Gong?

I must mention here, that this is an individual feeling not a one fit all. However, you must be aware that energy follows intent. When you place your awareness or consciousness to an area that is where the Qi will move to. You may experience the following sensations such as:

- Warm feeling,
- Coldness in the limbs, hands or body,
- Fullness,
- Tingling sensation,
- Numbness
- Heaviness in your limbs, fingers and hands.
- You may feel a magnetic sensation, like pulling or repelling.
- Sometimes you may feel a stubbing sensation in a specific part of your body, indicating that there is stagnation in the region. If you persist you will find that heat arrives to the region and that the stabbing sensation disappears and the Qi is able to flow smoothly.

You may find that when the back channels are blocked, your bladder and kidney organs may also be affected. The unblocking process takes a few weeks of continuous training at specific times in the evening to correlate to the organ affected. During the unblocking process you may feel many of the

above symptoms or effects. However, when the unblocking g of the bladder meridian occurs with Ba Duan Jin, you will find a desperate need to pass fluids. There may be a release of congeal blood or orange color in the urine then flowing to clear white flashing all stagnation and death cells out etc.

When practicing position one- *Supporting the Sky with Both Hands*- you may feel tingling running up the whole of your back and spine, this is a common sensation associated with the gathering of Qi in a particular area in your body or along the bladder meridian. Simply relax all your muscles to allow the Qi to flow. It is important that you place the tip of your tongue on the upper palate to ensure that a connection between the Du and Ren meridian exist allowing a continuous flow of energy.

陽氣

4 Warming Up Exercises

Here we will take a look at some simple warming up and cooling down exercises. These exercises are important in order to avoid soft tissue damage. It will also aid in the circulation of blood through the body in preparation for Ba Duan Jin. There are many ways to warm up and cool down, so this example is by no means a definitive solution. However, the chosen exercises will also help with the movement of Qi.

Warming Up Routine

This simple warming up exercises will help to limber up the muscles, maintain a free flow of energy and blood. It will benefit your joints, muscles, tendons, lungs and the circulatory system.

About Patting the Body

Patting the body is an ancient martial arts method of activating the Qi and blood. It helps to improve cardiopulmonary circulation; it helps to direct Qi to specific regions of the body activating the subcutaneous fascia along the musculotendinuous path.

The patting has to be done with the open palm in a calm and relaxed manner, with light force along the outside and inside of the

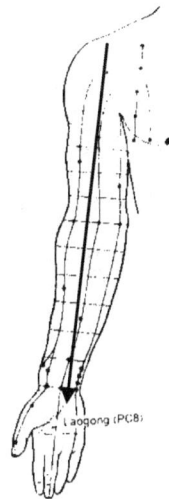

Laogong (PC8)

limbs, the lumbar region, gluteus, outside of your leg muscles all the way down to the calf muscles, return up by patting along the inner legs to the waist level.

The patting has to be done along the Qi direction flow according to the musculotendinuous area or meridian path that you are massaging. For example, when patting the inside of the arms, should be done in a downwards direction. When patting along he outside of the arms, pat in an upwards direction. Please refer back to the Three Yin Channels.

The Patting the Arms

The arms have three Yin and three Yang channels along the outside of the arm you have the Yang channels: Small Intestine, Sanjiao, and Large Intestine.

The Ying channels of the arm run downwards towards the fingers on the inner side of your arm, and it consist of three channels: Heart, Pericardium and lungs. You should exhale at point of contact. Patting along the inner side of the arm in a downwards direction towards the fingers.

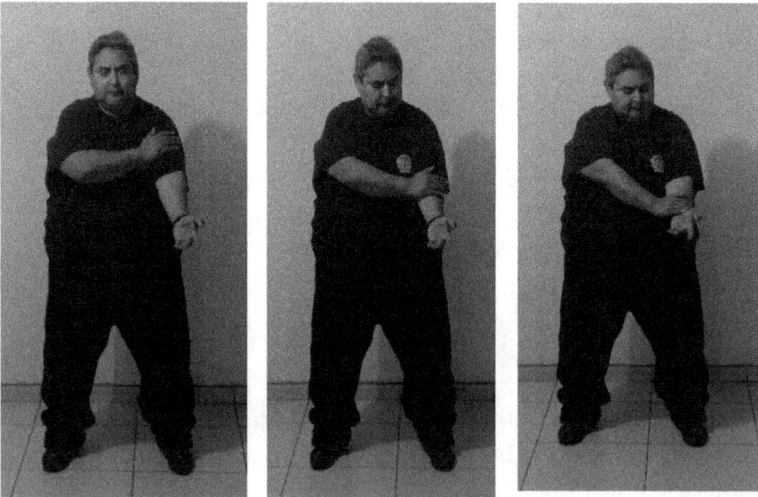

Patting the body helps to increase the blood circulation and Qi flow in the body. Thereby, reducing risks of blood clotting.

1. Patting upwards along the outside of the arm with the palms facing downwards.

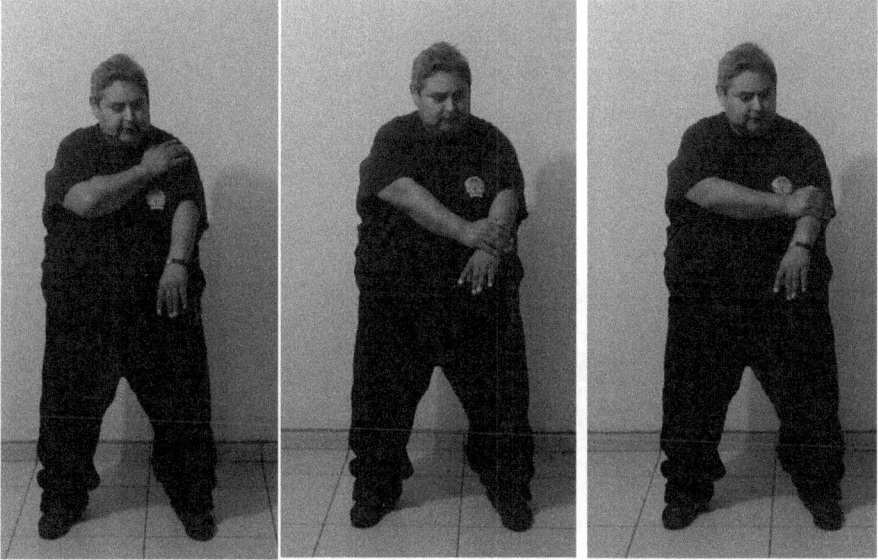

2. Then turning the hand over to repeat along the opposite side according the direction above. You can repeat three times the above sequences.

Patting the Torso

Patting downwards, along the side of the torso from the chest to lower abdomen to strengthen the Yang Qi. The kidney and stomach meridian run along the side of the body. The kidney runs upwards almost parallel to the sternum and the stomach meridian downwards along the center of the pectorals.

Pat gently along the stomach meridian, exhaling at point of impact, and inhaling in between each action. Repeat the same movements three times each, and then repeat to other side.

Patting the Lumbar Sacral Region

Gently patting the lumbar sacral region will activate the kidney function and increase blood circulation to that area. One of the largest meridians of the body passes through your back, the Urinary Bladder meridian relates to the bladder and the kidney vessel.

1. Place your palms behind your back at the level of your waist and gently patting your lower back and gluteus. Whilst, the other arm taps the lower abdomen, at the Qihai region, turn the waist as you reverse the arm positions. In effect this is knocking at the dantien and mingmen.

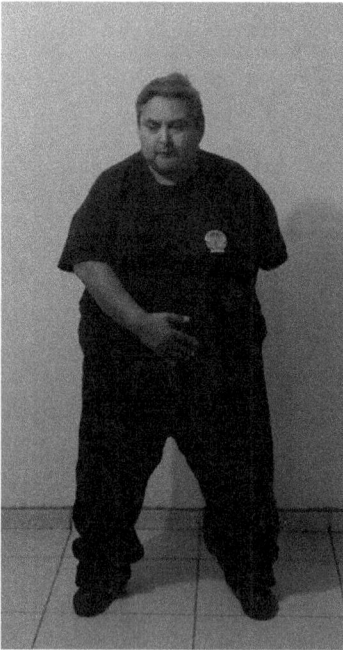

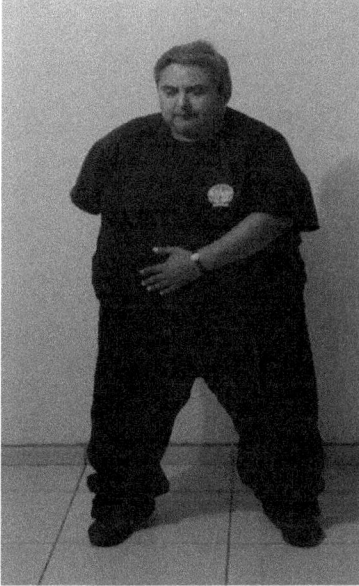

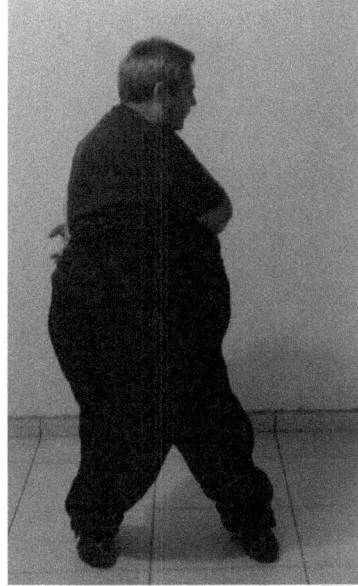

2. Exhale at point of contact, and repeat to other side three times each.

Patting the Legs

Continue to bend towards the ground, gently patting the back of your waist, legs from the gluteus to the Achilles tendon, then back up again the inner part of your legs to your groin area. And then repeat the whole sequence again from the top respectively.

Touching the feet is a simple exercise that requires a gentle tapping massage of your lumbar region, back of the legs all the way down to your feet. Once you reach your feet turn your palms in a circle over you instep and big toes, massaging along the inside of your legs as you stand up. One of its benefits is that it stretches your leg muscles, improves circulation and activates your kidneys.

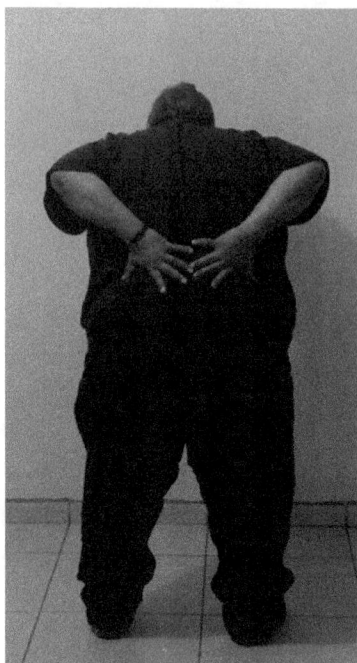
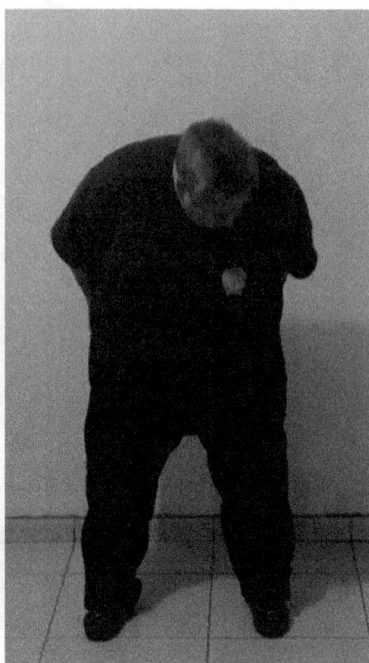
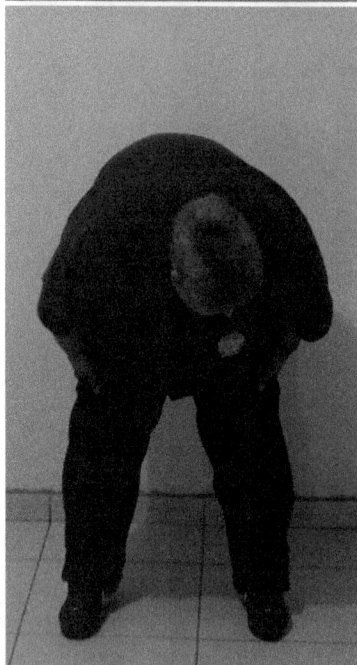
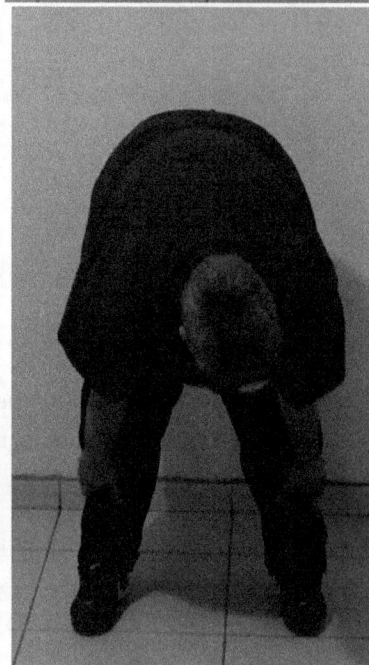

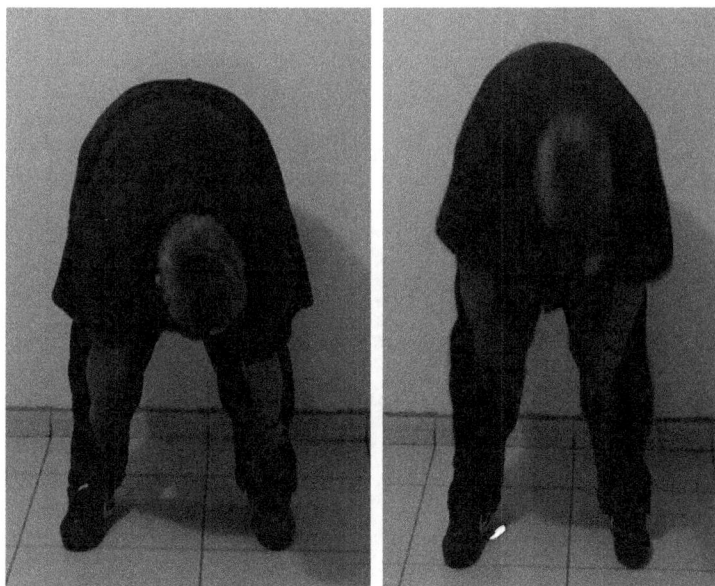

Sharpening an Axe

Sharpening the Axe is an exercise that raises the energy and helps to strengthen the structure and balance. Here it is important that you coordinate the inhaling and exhaling process with the movement to get the best benefit.

The action of the exercise is for you to imagine that you are holding an axe horizontally with both hands palms facing down. Now imagine you take one step forward with the right leg and you brace yourself, with one foot in front and the other behind shoulder width apart. You bend the knees slightly, imagine that you lift the axe horizontally and press forward slowly, transferring your weight toward the front knee.

As you begin to lift the axe from the waist to the abdomen level, you inhale, soft, smoothly and deep. At the point that you begin to shift you weight forward, you begin to exhale. The exhale should end together with the forward movement of the axe, when your arms are almost straight. One key point here is to keep your shoulders low and parallel, elbow tips pointing vertically down not horizontally outwards. The next stage is to relax at the end of the extension, inhale and slowly pull the axe horizontally backwards, when the hands are almost at your abdomen, sink your waist slowly press both hands down to the level of the bladder. Then you can repeat the same

41

movement again. Six times with the right leg forward, and then six with left leg forward, repeating the same process above. You will find the body would

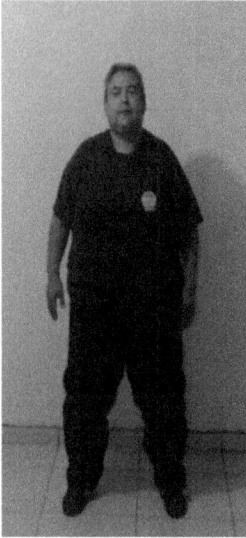

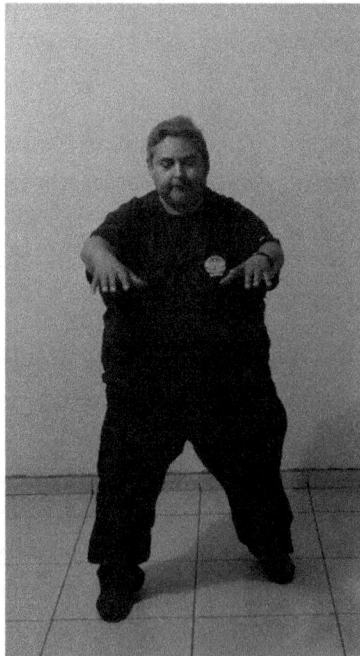

From the above position holding the axe out, in reality is a yin qi position which allows the vital energy to flow through all the yin meridians. When you do this exercise slowly and with intent you can feel the vital energy flow through the yin side and from between each finger. Ensure that you inhale slow and deep to the dantien pulling in the stomach as you inhale, when pushing out the arms exhale through the nose and expand the stomach walls.

Plucking an Apple

Compared to exercise two in the last page plucking an apple is by far more dynamic requiring deep abdominal breathing and vocalizing when exhaling as you sing your waist. It teaches you to lift the Qi and sink the Qi to the Dantien a point three fingers below the umbilicus. To proceed stand with right foot slightly in front shoulder width apart. Place both hands palms down in front of your thighs, begin inhale as you simultaneously raise both arms above your head and go into the ball of your feet. At this stage the inhaling is smooth, slow, deep and long. The inhaling terminates when your hand are vertically above your head and you are on the balls of your feet. Second stage, rotate your right wrist in a full small circle and imagine that you have grabbed an apple with your right hand and twist it, As you forcefully pull downwards stamp the heels of your feet onto the ground. The left palm presses downwards with force simultaneously, keeping the left palm at the level of the right elbow at all times. Sinking the waist as you stamp the ground and forcefully exhaling as you sink both, the left palm press and the right elbow downward press. Both arms move vertically downwards.

Do six complete movements as described above, then repeat the same sequence on the left side of the body.

Note: Rising onto the ball of the feet has the function of activating the kidney and bladder meridians and suddenly dropping your center of gravity to strike the ground brings Qi directly to your legs.

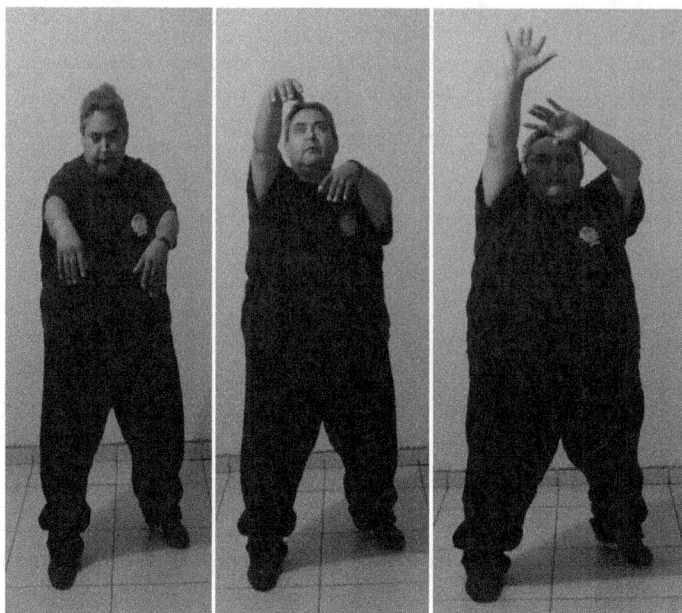

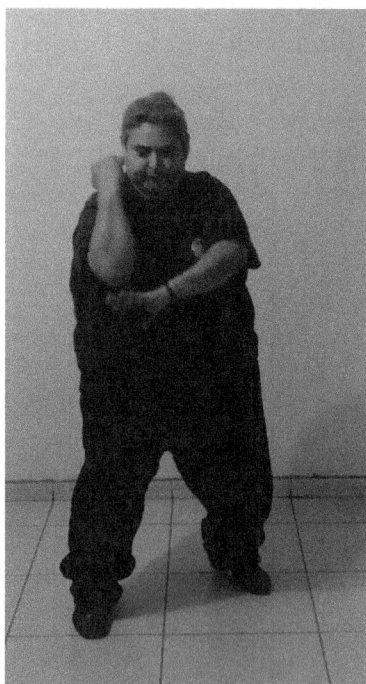

Gently Bouncing the Body

This exercise helps to realign the spinal process, internal viscera's and to direct vital energy to the legs. It has a strong effect on the kidneys and the spinal medulla. The main acupressure points involved here are the feet Yong Quan points (K1) and Shenshu (Bl23) Sanjiaoshu (Bl22). These latter two back points are stimulated by massage with palms to strengthen the kidneys and regulate the Sanjiao. Massage downwards from sanjiaoshu to shenshu, and then across.

Warm your hands then place your hand on top of your kidneys; rub as you inhale press slightly as you exhale directing the Qi to the kidneys and Qi Hai.

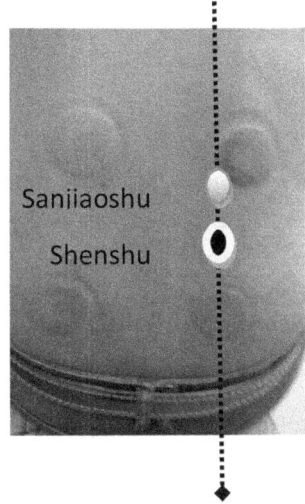

Saniiaoshu

Shenshu

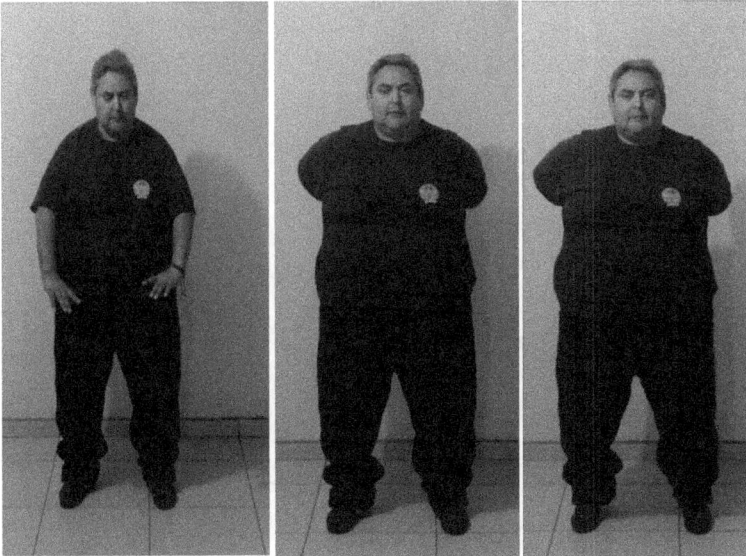

Squatting at Three Levels.

This exercise helps to strengthen the heart, the legs and increase knee joint flexibility and resistivity by increasing synovial fluid within the joint capsule. However, if you suffer from heart conditions you may avoid this exercise due to its demanding physical strain on the body. You must make sure that you are not out of breath, feeling weak, tired or dizzy when practicing to avoid unwanted side effects. Squatting at three levels implies having to bend the knees slightly at first, gradually doing a full squat as shown below. Once completed, slowly rise the body and repeat at least six times. You can use a chair for support if unable to do at first. Just bent the knees to a point where you feel comfortable. Breathe naturally, inhale as you begin and exhale as you squat. Inhale as you rise.

One of the benefits of this exercise is that it will benefit the Small Heavenly Circulation, that's when the Qi flows smoothly between the Ren and Du Mai of the Extra Ordinary Meridians; leading to strong protective Qi known as WeiQi.

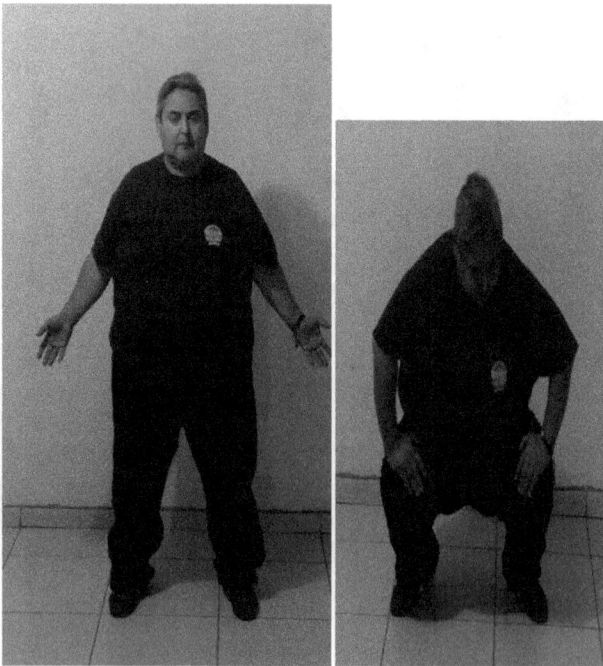

Turning the Wrist in a Tiger's Claw

As you now know there are three yin and three yang channels on the arms. The channels end and begin at the finger tips of each hand, so as previously mentioned inside of the arms and hands are yin and the outside are considered yang. So, the Tiger's Claw restrains the Yin Qi, pushing the energy from the fingers to the internal organs in relation to the three Yin and three Yang channels and related organs. The Tiger Claw either opens or closes the pertaining organs to the fingers by rotating the wrists and forming the tiger claw.

The breathing pattern also influences the opening and closing of the meridians endpoints and related internal organs.

The thumb area where LI4 is found and the thumb endpoint where the lung meridian terminates influences and reflects the spleen (Earth element).

The index finger itself contains the Large Intestine meridian endpoint but it reflects the liver organ (wood element). The middle finger contains the pericardium meridian endpoint which reflects the heart (Fire element) energetically. Whilst the ring finger also contains the sanjiao meridian endpoint, but it reflects the lungs (metal); the little finger contains the heart and small intestine meridians endpoints but reflects the kidneys (water element) energetically.

By forming a tiger claw, the meridians endpoint and finger areas can help to balance the whole body. That's why in traditional kung fu they speak of gripping with your toes as well and forming a tiger's claw to develop strength. For further information regarding the Wuxing or Five elements see Chapter 2

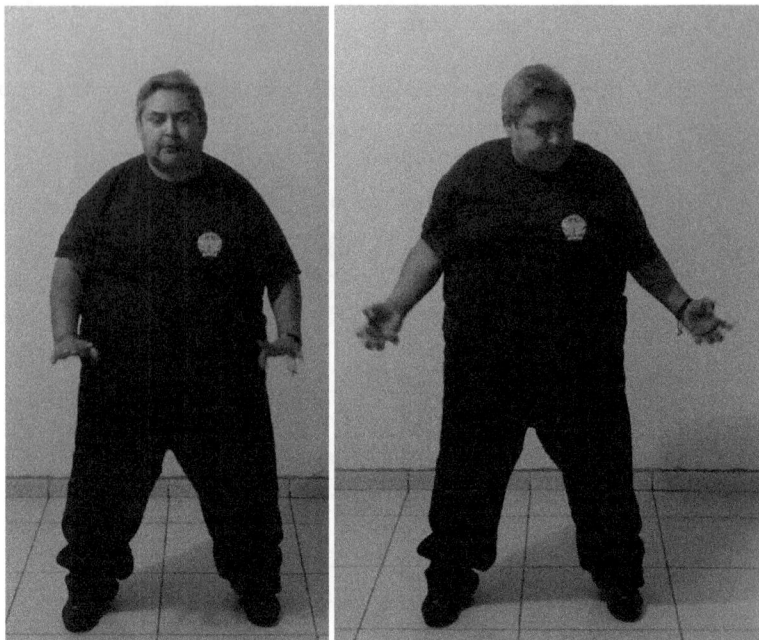

5 THE EIGHT STRAND OF BROCADE

Description to exercises:

Ba Duan Jin Qi Gong consists of eight basic positions and they all emanate from the Wu-Chi position. This position is a state of emptiness, where you focus on your inner-self, and ignore or put aside external conflicts. It will help you to relax your body and to calm your mind and emotions. It allows you to enter the correct frame of mind, prior to commencing the Eight Golden Silk Exercises.

Body Alignment

In order to successfully achieve the above, it is important to align not only the skeletal structure but also the three points: Bai Hui, Hui Yin and the two Yong Quan points (Kidney1 point) of the feet.

The best way to align the structure is as described above. However, to ensure that Bai Hui and Hui Yin points are align above each other you have to slightly round your back, drop your shoulders and tack in your tail bone slightly. The Yong Quan points are on the sole of you feet, you need to ensure that when you slightly bend your knees the sole of the feet are flat on the floor especially at the kidney 1 point. You Head aligns with your tail bone and your shoulders with your waist.

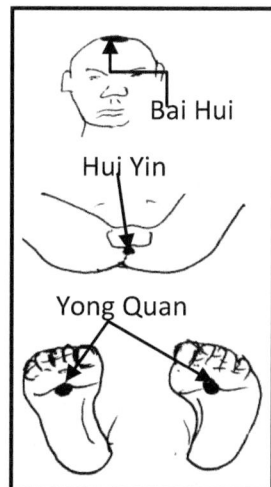

Bai Hui

Hui Yin

Yong Quan

The Wu-Chi Position

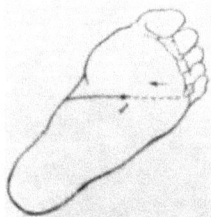

Place feet shoulder width apart and parallel. Knees soft not locked straight and pointing forward to the toes. Pelvis slightly tucked under. Top of the head suspended from above with chin slightly tucked under. Shoulders and upper ribs in a relaxed state, with arms hanging to the sides with fingers facing thighs (Shoulders relax and hanging naturally). Look straight ahead, half close your eyes to gain concentration, breathe in and out through the nose directing the breath to the lower abdomen. Relax and be comfortable. Breathe deeply and slowly, with tip of tongue touching the upper ridge of your teeth (upper palate).

When you are in this position as shown aside, you will feel a sense of calmness, your body will feel light, and your arms would want to lift by themselves. It is like if you are at one with nature. At this point you can begin to practice Ba Duan Jin absorbing Yin Qi. Everything begins and ends in the Wu-chi position; therefore it is imperative that you enter a relaxed estate of mind, releasing all tension. Even if you were to practice Wu-Chi for 29 minutes every day you will rip good health benefits and stress free.

1. Supporting the Sky with Both Hands

This position regulates all the internal organs, by regulating the San Jiao (discussed in previous chapter); this has a direct effect on the heart, lungs, spleen, kidneys, liver, pancreas and intestines. Raising the arms to regulate the San Jiao can relieve fatigue, increase inhalation and invigorate the muscles and bones of your back and waist. Additionally, it enhances the blood movement through your body, improving your Qi circulation. By raising the arms over the head the six yin and six yang channels of your arms are stimulated. If you were to lift the heels gently off the ground as you stretch the arm over the head, the Kidney channel is further stimulated, enhancing kidney function and kidney Qi via point Yong Kuan (K1 point in last chapter, and shown aside). From wu-chi position, link fingers & inhale whilst lifting hands above head, drop & tuck in chin, press with palm-heel, exhale & return to original position. Repeat this movement six times. (6x)

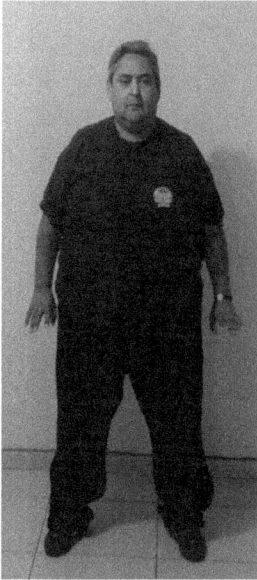

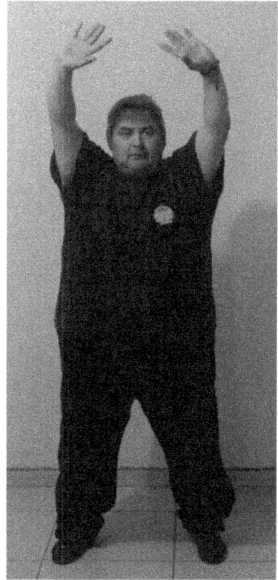

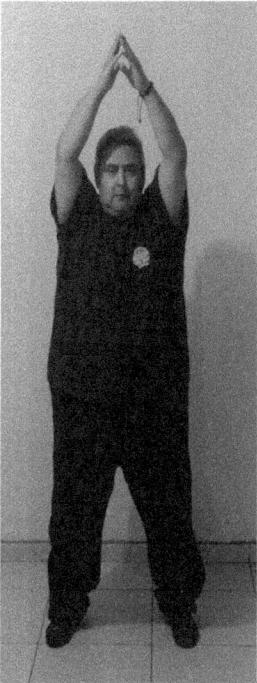

2. Drawing a bow to the left and right

This position tends to regulate the function of the Liver and Lungs, regulating the upper San Jiao. When lifting the bow to the left the liver is stimulated, as we subconsciously direct the Qi to the liver. When lifting the bow to the right the lung is stimulated as we use the lungs to sink the Qi. When you slightly twist your waist you activate the paravertebral muscles (a group of muscles that run vertically parallel to the spinal column) stimulating the kidney via the bladder meridian strengthening the lumbar region. To assume the position step left, then right alternately into a small horse stance by bending the knees; inhale draw bow & exhale. Repeating three times to both sides.

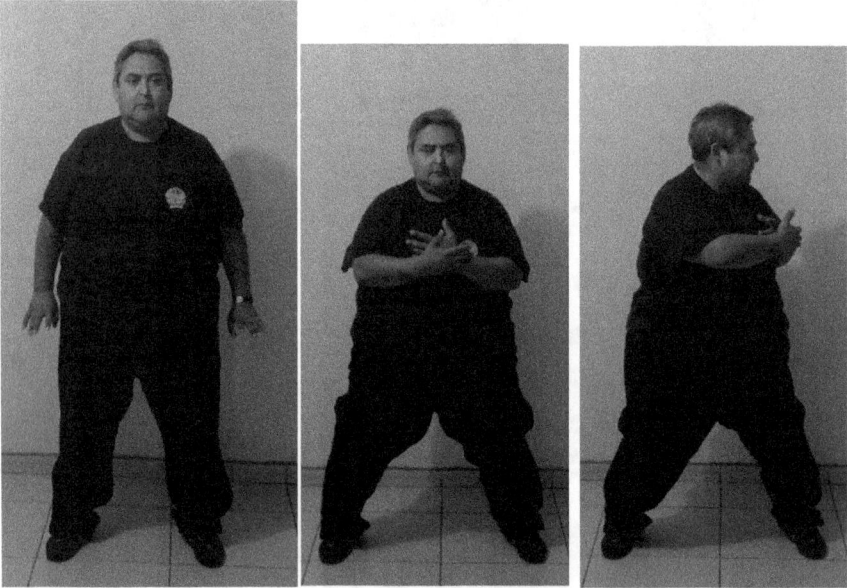

3. Lifting one arm up to the sky to regulate the Spleen & Stomach Function.

This position regulates the function of the spleen and stomach. It moves the spleen Qi up and the stomach Qi downwards, regulating the flow of Qi on both sides of the body. Therefore, achieving balance between yin and yang.

The balance is obtained as you lift one hand over the head to gather heavenly Qi and simultaneously press the other downwards towards the ground to gather earth Qi. Absorbing earth Qi via the Yong Quan points (K1); and heavenly Qi through Laogong points in the center of your palms (PC8). The overall effect is an improve function to the gall bladder, liver, spleen and stomach. Additionally, it can improve and to some extend prevent gastro intestinal track problems.

From the wu-chi position lift both palms face up to the level of the chest. Push left hand slowly above head and inhale, straighten up simultaneously pushing up-wards with Left palm and pressing downwards with right palm. Exhale and return to starting Wu-chi position and repeat with other side six times.

In ancient times this particular exercise was considered as tiger and dragon breath.

Where the Qi of the chest is considered as fire or tiger breathe. Whilst, the Qi from the stomach is considered as water or dragon breathe. The actual mixing of the 'water and fire' as you know, it causes steam to be formed. The steam here represents the word Qi itself. Therefore, Qi is able to create more energy in the body.

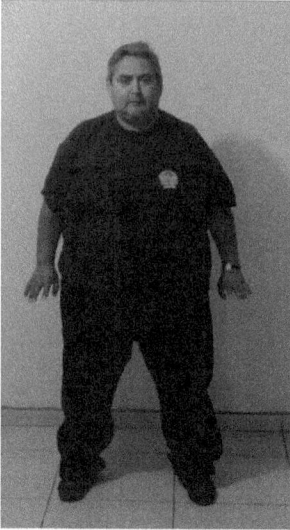

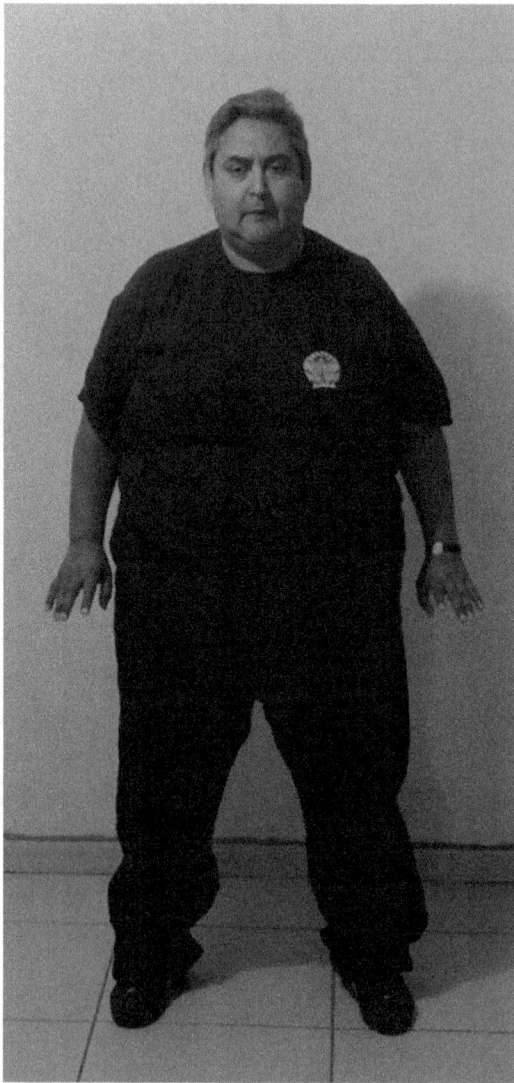

4. Ox-looking at the moon to reduce sickness and stress

Ox- Looking at the Moon like the first exercise is a very powerful set. It strongly acts on the central nervous system and the circulation of blood and vital energy to the head, helping to regulate the cerebral-cortex.

The turning of the waist and head helps to activate the musculoskeletal system, stretching the paravertebral muscles, upper trapezium and neck muscles. This further activates the bladder and kidney vessels and the sanjiao. One of the main benefits of this exercise is to help reduce high blood pressure and harden arteries.

From the Wu-Chi position, center your body, straighten up, inhale, drop shoulders, spread arms, lift palms to Middle Dan Tien, slowly sink palms to waist as you gently turn the waist and head to look behind and up.

Exhale, then return arms to lower Dan Tien level and repeat to other side as described previously, repeat three times each left and right movement.

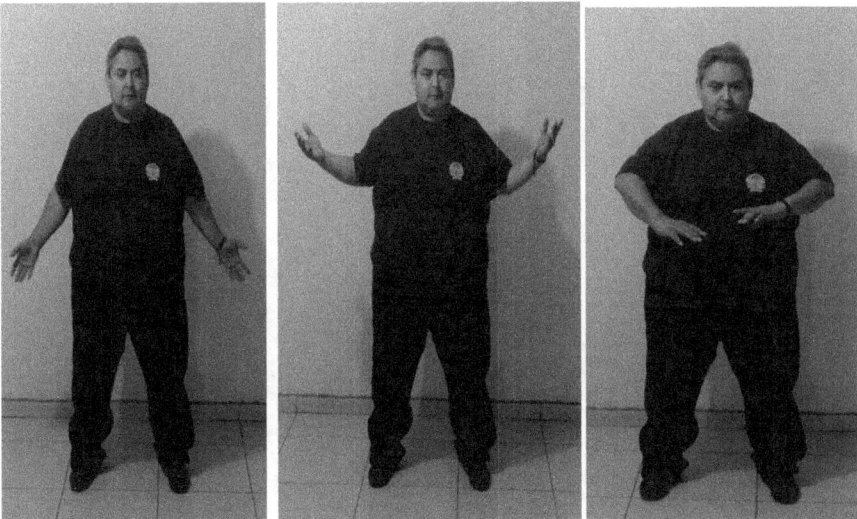

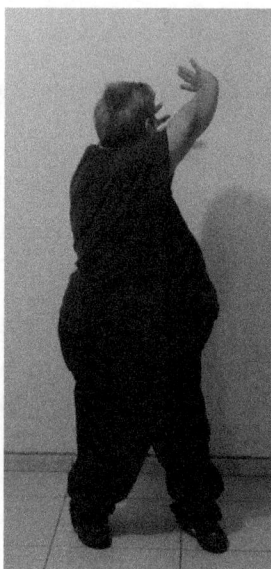

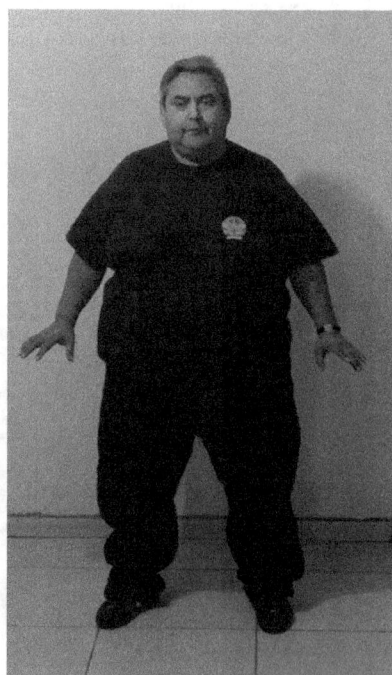

5. Lowering the head and hip to relieve excess heat from Heart & stress

Bending & Stretching the Waist to relieve excess heat from the heart. Raise your right hand over your head above Bai Hui pressure point, transfer your weight towards your right leg, bending to the side over your left leg, rising slightly your left heal off the ground. Your left arm slides down on the outside of your left leg, massaging your Gall Bladder Channel on the left side and stretching your spleen channel on your right side.

Inhale as you lift your hand up, exhale as you go down. To complete the set, you inhale as you return to the starting position. Repeat both left and right sides three times.

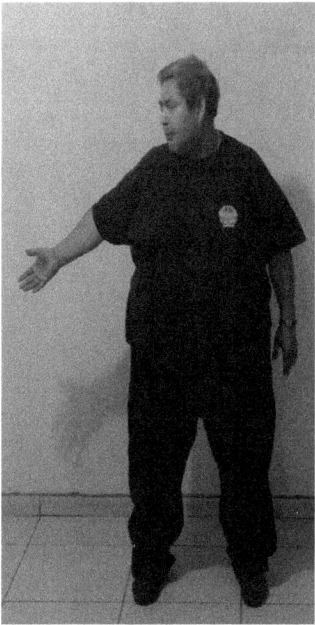

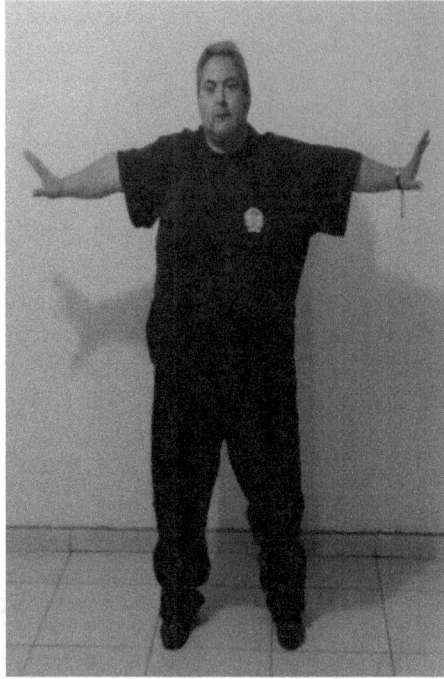

6. Touching the feet and moving the tail to strengthen kidneys

From the Wu-chi position simultaneously lift both palms upward towards the head, with palms facing forward. Look straight ahead. Gently press the palms down to the front of your chest and then bring the hands to the side of your spine moving your palms downwards towards the back of your hips as if you are massaging the sides of the spine as your hands slide down.

Bring your upper body forward as you are doing this, to form a 90 degrees angle. This helps to stretch the spine and strengthen the kidneys, whilst, simultaneously rubbing the back of your thighs with your palms, until you reach the top of your insteps. Hold this posture for a minute looking forward and ahead. Then move both palms forwards along the floor, then to left and right before lifting your arms, bending your knees slowly as you squat down, massaging you knee joints from outside to inside, gently straightening your body as you stand up, arching your back to open you chest, at the Zhongwan point and fully exhaling to release stagnant Qi from the heart, or excess heat. Repeat this sequence six times. Overall, this stimulates the Bladder, Du and Sanjiao meridian. Stimulating acupressure points: Ming Men (GV4), Yaoyangguan (GV3), Weizhong (BL40) and Laogong (PC8).

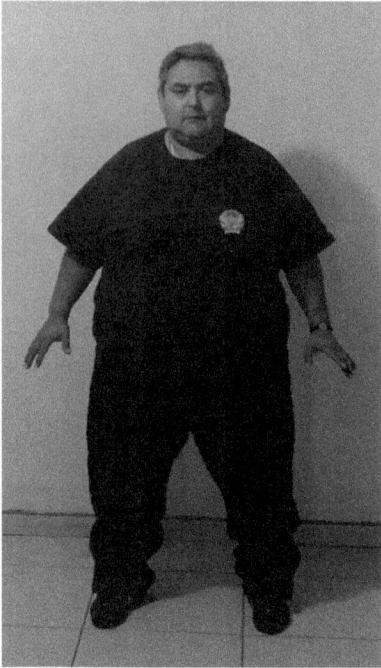

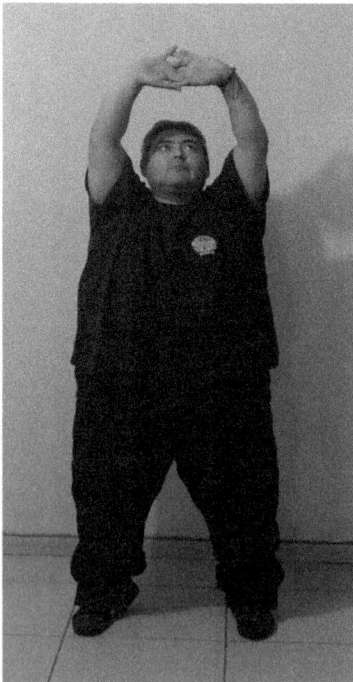

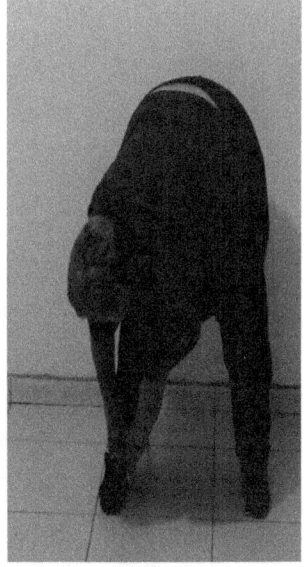

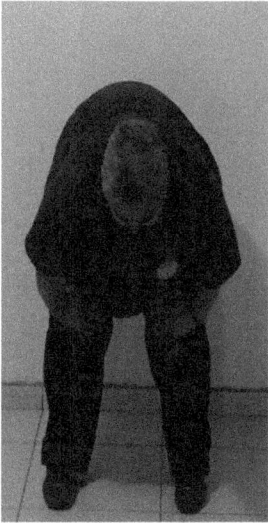

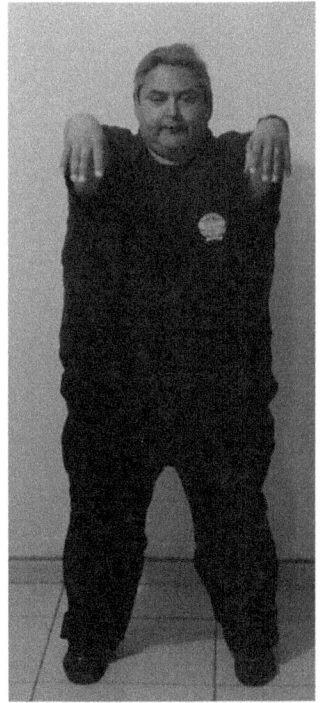

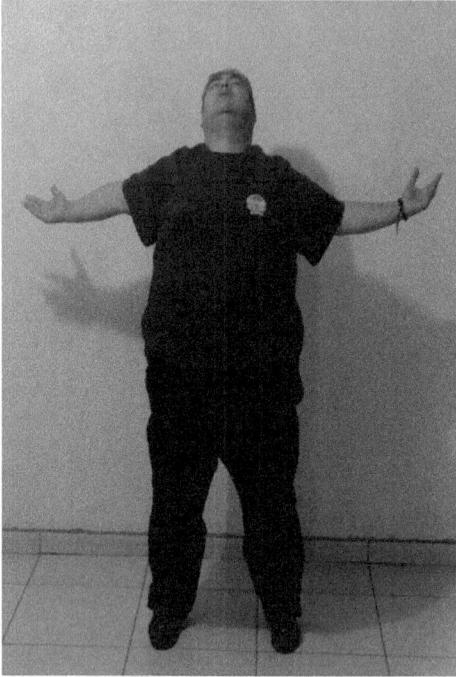 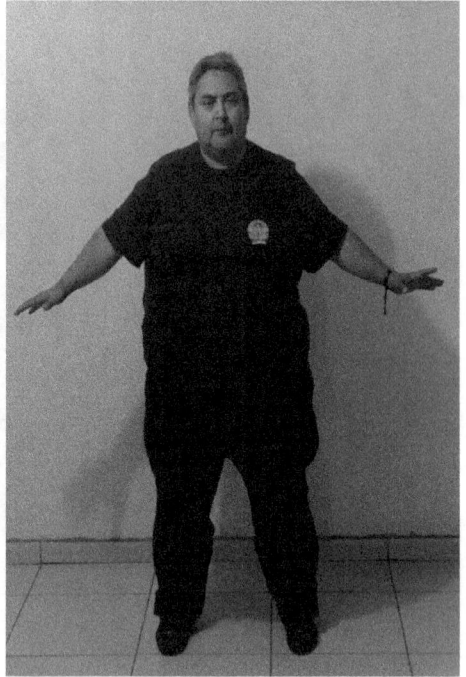

7. Punching & Glaring Forcibly to Enhance Strength.

From the ready position, shift the weight to the right and move the left foot to the side to form a horse-riding stance. Gently grasp your thumb with your fingers as if clenching your fist. Make upright fists by the waist and punch slowly and forcibly with your left fist, whilst glaring and exhale. Open and extend fingers, rotate wrists counter-clockwise and imaging you are grasping or catching a wrist, inhaling at the same time. Withdraw the fist to the side of the waist and repeat the punching action with the right. Repeat this process three times. In Chinese medicine it is believed that the liver channel controls muscles and tendons and that the eyes are connected with the liver. Therefore, from the martial arts point of view it is believed that a strong glare represents intent, Blood and Qi circulation. This exercise then can strengthen your muscles and overall power. It can also help to regulate excess Qi from the liver.

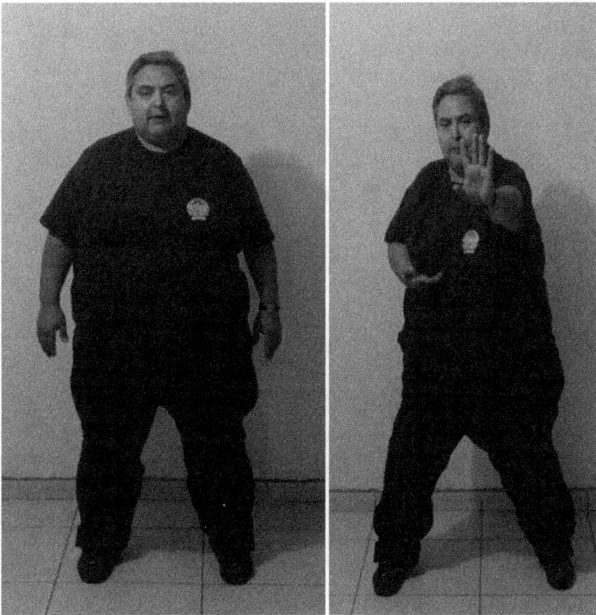

8. Shaking the body cure diseases

Bring feet together, with ankles and thighs touching, keep your shoulders down and head erect, inhale and rise slowly on your toes to maximum extension (pull in abdomen, buttocks and chin). Hold briefly with teeth clenched, drop backwards onto heels and exhale. Repeat three to six times. The action of raising and tapping the heels on the ground can help to activate the Bladder, Sanjiao, Du Mai, Liver, Spleen and Kidney meridians, which in turn help to regulate the function of the related organs, in as well as gently massaging them, and stimulating the joints and spine. Also the vibrating of the spine helps to gently re-align the spinal column sending the Qi down to the legs.

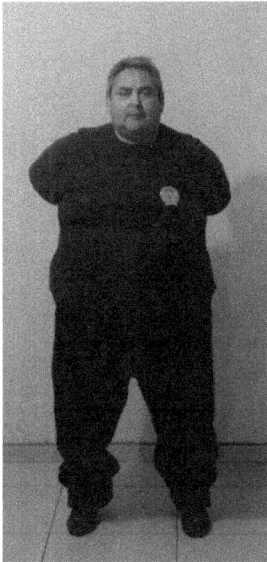

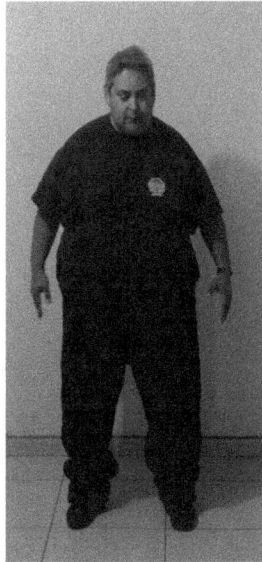

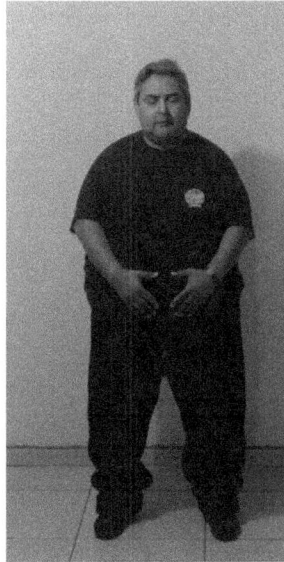

Closing

Finally, relax the body; bring your hands back towards your lumbar region. Place your hands on the kidneys, inhale as you lift your heels massaging your kidneys as you bring your heels down slowly exhale, directing the Qi to the lower Dan Tien. Repeat six times.

Stand naturally with hands folded on Dan Tien and breathe naturally for a few minutes. Dan Tien expanding and contacting as you exhale and inhale respectively.

6 ACUPUNCTURE POINTS IN BA DUAN JIN

The following table lists the most important points within the Ba Duan Jin Qi Gong form.

Acupuncture Point	Location	Meridian	Related Organ
Yong Quan (K1)	Base of foot	Kidney	Kidney
Laogong (PC8)	Center of palm	Pericardium	Spleen & stomach
Bai Hui (GV20)	Crown of Head	Du Mai	Brain
Ming Men (GV4)	Small of back-3rd lumbar vertebra	Du Mai	Gate of life
Weizhong (BL40)	Behind the knee joint	Bladder	Kidney
Sanjiaoshu (BL22)	Resides second lumbar vertebra	Bladder	Kidney
Shenshu (BL23)	One inch below sanjiaoshu BL22	Sanjiao	Kidney
Dan Tien	2 inches Below umbilicus	Ren Mai	Sea of Energy
Yangguan (GV3)	Upper sacral region	Du Mai	Spine
Dazhui (GV14)	1st Thoracic vertebra	Du Mai	Brain ,spine
HUI YING (CV1)	Perineum	Ren Mai	Sea of Yin

Combination sequences to ease certain diseases

1. If you combine set 1, set 2 and set 8 together it can help ladies suffering from postmenstrual syndrome (PMS).
2. Combine set 1 and set 6 to open blocked bladder meridian
3. Combine set 2, set 3, and set 5 to reduce high blood pressure
4. Combine set 1, set 2 and set 4 to activate cerebral cortex and improve concentration and relaxation.

ABOUT THE AUTHOR

Eduardo Barrios was born in Valparaiso, Chile 1965. He is a respected traditional Chinese Martial Arts instructor and practitioner of Chinese Acupuncture. His background in Southern Praying Mantis Kung Fu, Tui Na, Dit Da and external trauma herbs was obtained from his mentor Grand Master Ho Kung Wah over seven years training as his apprentice and under Professor Li Yia Qin five years Qi Gong training.

In 1991, whilst at Southbank University, he had the opportunity to meet Professor Li Yia Qin, whilst there he learns various Qi Gong forms such as Ba Duan Jin, Fragrance Qi Gong, Zhuan Zhang Qi Gong, and meditation and Qi Gong massage methods.

Eduardo is an accomplished alternative therapist, having completed his post-graduate level diploma studies in Orthopaedic Acupuncture and Micro-Systems at the College of Chinese Medicine under the guidance of Paul Robin, accredited by the Acupuncture Society. Eduardo has also trained under John Tindall, one of the leading exponents of Auricular Acupuncture Micro-Systems in the UK and Director of NADA GB. Eduardo trained in the NADA Protocol and the Master Auricular Acupuncture course at the Yuan Clinic & Traditional Medicine College.

Eduardo is planning to run his own private clinic, practicing Orthopaedic Acupuncture and Micro-Systems, applying NADA protocol and Dit Da massage to help individuals suffering from acute and chronic pain.

www.ingramcontent.com/pod-product-compliance
Lightning Source LLC
LaVergne TN
LVHW051708080426
835511LV00017B/2792